WOMEN ARE HERE TO STAY

THE DURABLE SEX IN ITS INFINITE VARIETY

THROUGH HALF A CENTURY

OF AMERICAN LIFE

BY
AGNES ROGERS

ΛΑΜ ΠΑΔΙΑ
ΕΧΟ ΝΤΕΣ
ΔΙΑ ΔΩΣΟΥΣΙΝ

Α ΛΛΗΛΟΙΣ

HARPER & BROTHERS PUBLISHERS NEW YORK

WOMEN ARE HERE TO STAY

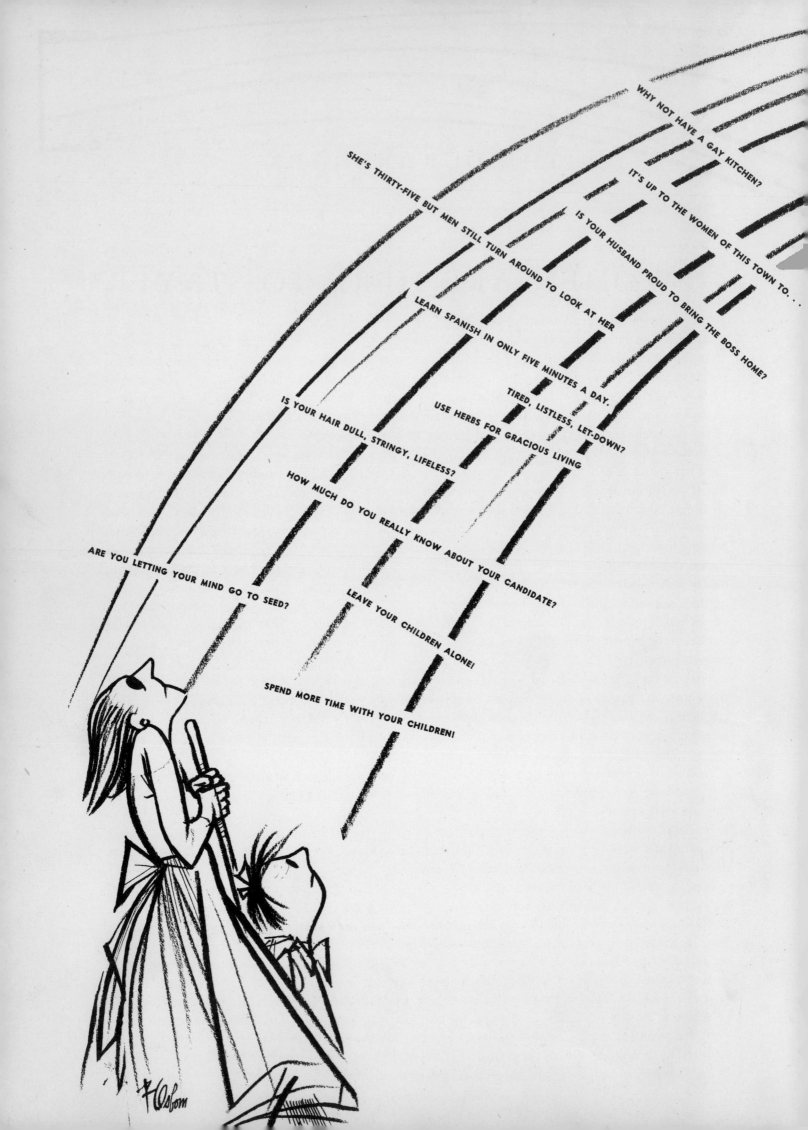

THE DURABLE SEX

There have been so very many books written at and about women that one might wonder why anybody should want to add another to the list.

Women have been the subject—collectively and individually—of most of the poetry and songs of the world, and what artists and sculptors would do without them it is hard to imagine. They have been praised (not recently, to be sure), exhorted, scolded, pitied, and explained until you'd think there was nothing left to say on the subject. Heads have been shaken over them and fingers wagged at them from St. Paul to Ferdinand Lundberg.

American women in particular have been the target of the harshest criticism: they are accused of strangling their children with silver cords, of making miserable their husbands with their greed, extravagance, and irresponsibility, and, indeed, of corrupting the fine vigor of their country's traditions by their soft and deadly influence. Momism, the woman who henpecks her husband, and the wife in control of the family purse are purely American concepts. (Incidentally, these guilty creatures are the object of ardent envy on the part of most women of other countries.)

Along with this stream of criticism there runs a mighty river of advice and admonition. No sooner have her critics proved that the miserable offender is unworthy to live, than they demand of her an all-round perfection that would be nothing short of miraculous. The American woman today must be an expert housekeeper, doing all of the cooking, washing, and cleaning with skill, dispatch, and good humor (and why not, with all those fine household machines at her command!). She must be a wise, conscientious, and loving mother, always there when the children need her, but standing aside when her presence might threaten the full development of their individuality. She must be a delightful, helpful, thrifty wife, ready to administer comfort or to share in gay adventure. She must be a useful member of the community, informed on broad political trends as well as possible danger spots in the local school board. She is also a citizen of the world and should be able to name the current President of France, have constructive ideas on what to do with the atom bomb, and say what's wrong with our foreign policy.

That isn't all. She is expected to read, look at, listen to the important new books, pictures, music, for women are the traditional guardians of culture. If she's young, she should be cultivating some interest against the time when the children don't need her. If she's old, she should be happily occupied in some moderately useful, unspectacular fashion, keeping herself decently to herself, and not interfering with her juniors and betters.

And at all times, and at all ages, she should be, if not actually beautiful, as good-looking as perfect grooming, a disciplined figure, and good clothes can make her. (This part is very easy. The advertisements tell you how.)

It would not be surprising if women gave up entirely, crushed by the barrage of abuse and advice, and paralyzed by the impossible goals set for them. They don't, though. They keep on living—longer than men, as a matter of fact. It is, indeed, a durable sex.

Now in nearly all books about women, the authors assume that women think and act first of all as women, not as individuals, and this assumption leads into the habit of thinking that they're all pretty much alike. It is my intention to demonstrate that there are a great many different kinds of women (just as there are a great many different kinds of men) and that it is almost impossible to generalize about them—tempting though this may be, and very good fun as a pastime. I even believe that in most cases the Colonel's lady has more in common with the Colonel than with Judy O'Grady.

In this book you will find a large variety of women. Some of your favorites aren't here in person because the book is not a *Who's Who*. I am not trying to summarize "women's accomplishments," since that seems to imply that women have a life of their own apart from the rest of the body politic. I am trying to indicate various concepts and patterns of behavior that have influenced American life in the past fifty years or so, with especial regard to their impact upon women. A.R.

THE SHELTERED LADY

In such an atmosphere as this, the sheltered lady, Victorian ideal of perfect womanhood, grew and flourished. The charming portrait of the Hatch family was painted by Eastman Johnson in 1871. The women of the eighteen-nineties who belonged to prosperous American families were born into homes very much like this, and the young lady on the opposite page may very well have taken part in such a scene eighteen years earlier as a well-behaved baby.

The portrait illustrates the large family, the mingling of the generations, the comfortable spacious interior, the paternal watchfulness (Mr. Hatch, at the desk, is obviously asking his son John, at the door, hat in hand, where he's going)—all characteristics of comfortable American life of the period. And Mrs. Hatch, standing by the mantel, how graceful she is, how composed. American manners were based largely on the European (chiefly English) pattern, but because of our pioneer experience in which the family was a self-sufficient unit to be preserved at all costs, the American woman was placed on a pedestal even higher than in Victorian England. Practically all European visitors to this country in the mid-nineteenth century expressed astonishment at the extreme deference paid to women.

The young lady at the right is correctly dressed for calling or promenading. We may be sure of one thing, she is not on her way to or from the office. In 1889, when this picture was taken, the unmarried daughter was concerned with the "finer things of life," social amenities, travel, the arts (in a modest way). If the family fortunes failed, she might become a teacher, and it would be up to the more prosperous relations to treat her with every kindness.

Fifth Avenue, New York, in 1898, was a scene of considerable elegance according to W. T. Smedley's painting. You are looking north toward Central Park. The farthest building on the left is the imposing house of Mr. Cornelius Vanderbilt. Two men on the box mark a well turned out carriage, and you will notice that the women walking are all holding up their skirts, correctly, not incorrectly.

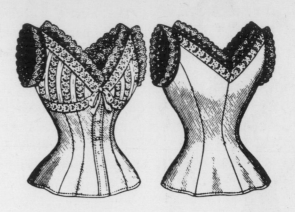

All of the illustrations on these two pages of fashions of the mid-nineties are McCall patterns, published in *The Queen of Fashion,* a woman's magazine which later became *McCall's.* At the left, above, is a tailor-made costume described as a Military Jacket with Eton effect. "The tailor-made costumes," says the magazine (September 1894), "are not only the most sensible and suitable costumes for everyday wear in public places, but there is an air of quietly correct style about them that commends them to general favor." Although the skirt appears to clear the ground, it still has to be held up when the wearer is walking outdoors (see page 3). In *The Queen of Fashion* for October 1895 there is a short article entitled "How to Hold Up a Dress." In it the reader is told, "In the days when three yards was a good width for a dress, a deft twitch of the hand sufficed to raise the skirt sufficiently; nowadays one must clutch the vexatious fullness which eludes even the most skilled hand. . . . To raise a skirt successfully requires practice. Place the right hand well around to the back and gather up the folds carefully, taking care not to lift the skirt too high. . . . The present style makes one reckless; either the dress is allowed to drag or ineffectual efforts are made to hold it up, resulting in disaster and ruin." The evening dress at the left (February 1896) is made of white satin brocaded with large pink flowers, with trimmings of lace, jeweled passementerie, and ribbon garnitures. For the corset cover at the top of the page, the combination corset cover and open drawers below, and the nightgown on page 5, nainsook or fine batiste were the favored materials. Ladies wore hand-made underclothes and spent a good deal of time running baby ribbon through the beading around the top, since it had to be removed when the garments were washed.

The bicycle costume at the right (August 1894) won the New York *Herald's* prize of $50 for the best design combining comfort and safety. Dark blue storm serge is suggested, with scarlet cashmere for the chemisette and sash. Leggings of tan leather are preferred, and instead of the Turkish fez shown, a college cap or a sailor might be substituted, but nothing more fancy.

Mohair or flannel were the customary fabrics for bathing suits in 1895, but in the same issue (July) in which the suit at the right was shown, an editorial in *The Queen of Fashion* pointed out that "The *elegantes* who frequent Atlantic City and Narragansett Pier often use silk." The article ran on to say, "Swimming has become a favorite pastime of society. Mrs. August Belmont, Mrs. C. Oliver Iselin (of yachting fame), Mrs. DeLancey Kane, the Misses Sloane are but a few out of many of New York's *grandes dames* who are adepts in the natatorial art."

One is mildly surprised in looking over fashion notes of the nineties to see how many different gradations of clothes were necessary: simple costumes for morning shopping, more elaborate ones for calling, still more elaborate if one drove to pay the calls, and different degrees of dressiness for theatre-going, depending on whether one sat in the orchestra or in a box. The tea gown, shown below, "is just the thing to put on when one comes home tired and weary from an afternoon's shopping or visiting.

The Queen of Fashion for May 1896 refers to Mrs. William Astor, whose portrait appears above, as the widowed American millionaire who gives the most famous dinner parties, and mentions the fact that for these she always dresses in black velvet. The magazine states that occasionally, when Mrs. Astor's dinners are for younger members of society, she may serve only twelve courses, but that when veterans of society are the main guests, the full twenty courses are invariably served. Mrs. Astor was the acknowledged ruler of New York society —and thus, in a sense, of American society—in the eighties.

Mrs. O. H. P. Belmont, the former Mrs. W. K. Vanderbilt, at the right, is indulging in the fashionable pastime of coaching. Mrs. Belmont, though possessed of a secure place in New York society, was nonetheless vigorous in the battle for women's rights, thus straying from the pattern of the sheltered lady to a marked degree.

The fashionable group below, who are attending a wedding in the 1903-05 period, illustrate the kind of people who were thought worth writing about in the general magazines of the eighties and nineties, and indeed until World War I. Not that society columns do not still continue, and are not still read with great interest, but the doings of the socially elect are no longer considered of as vital interest to practically everybody as they once were.

Jay Gould, at the height of his speculative career, in 1881, bought a fine house on Fifth Avenue, New York, at 47th Street. The photograph at the left shows the library and demonstrates the fact that the wealthy of the time, like nature, abhorred a vacuum.

Fine New York—and other city—houses had a ballroom as a matter of course. The photograph below was taken in the ballroom of the house belonging to Edmund Lincoln Baylies at 369 West 28th Street, New York, when that address was presumably more fashionable than it is today.

The Vanderbilts, as a family, were given to large and lavish houses, and in the Cornelius Vanderbilt mansion the late nineteenth century's fondness for the Turkish corner was expanded into the production of a whole Turkish room.

The big houses of the period were ideally suited for entertaining, but no social event of the time outshone the wonderful ball given in Mr. William K. Vanderbilt's new house—on Fifth Avenue at 52nd Street—on March 26, 1883. For one thing, it established the Vanderbilts in New York society's inner circle. Despite their wealth, the family had not had the formal approval of that social monarch, Mrs. Astor, but Miss Carrie Astor was so confident that she would be invited to the ball that she organized a quadrille among her friends for the occasion. Learning of this, Mrs. Vanderbilt murmured to a friend her regret that she could not invite Miss Astor since her mother had never called. The hint bore fruit. Mrs. Astor called.

The ball was front page news in the *New York Times*, and one article on it said: "The seasons bring the flowers again, and Easter brings the new bonnets, but not the bonnets alone. It brings to that unemployed pleasure-seeking society relaxation from the restraints of Lent and countless expectations of enjoyment, and ushers in a round of entertainments all the more rapid in procession and delirious in excitement for the long season of fasting and self-denial which has gone before." The estimated expenses of the ball were impressive: $250,000 was said to be the total cost, with $11,000 for the flowers, $155,730 for the costumes, $65,270 for the champagne, etc.

The accounts of the costumes worn at the Vanderbilt ball made heady reading. Miss Kate Strong, at the left, came as a cat, as you can see at a glance. White cat tails ornamented her full skirt, a blue ribbon with a golden bell and the name "Puss" on it encircled her neck, and the headdress was described as "a stiffened white cat's skin, the head over the forehead and the tail pendant behind." Below is a group of guests in Russian dress. Other costumes were described by the *Times* as follows: "Miss Kate Bulkley will congeal into ice; Miss Turnure will be transformed into an Egyptian princess; Miss Beckwith will twinkle as a fixed star; Miss Marion Langdon will soar as a golden butterfly, while one of her ardent admirers will pursue her as an entomologist; Mrs. Frank White will, in a picturesque woolly costume, disguise herself as a mountain sheep."

The James Hazen Hyde costume ball of January 31, 1905, was another memorable social event. For the occasion, Sherry's was transformed into a miniature Versailles and the guests came as ladies and gentlemen of the eighteenth-century French court. Mme Réjane, shown below emerging from a sedan chair, was imported from Paris, together with a French company, who entertained the guests with two little French plays. A ballet was performed by Mlle Varesi supported by dancers from the Metropolitan Opera, and a contra dance was staged by debutantes of the season and their escorts. This was the last of the sensationally great balls. Public resentment of great fortunes, kindled by the muckrakers, was further fanned by such examples of conspicuous waste, and the rich prudently moderated the extravagance of their entertainments.

An example of intimate entertaining is shown above at a bridesmaids' dinner given in 1904. You will notice the pink-shaded candlesticks, the lavish display of silver on the sideboard, and the baronial style of decoration then considered suitable for the dining-room.

THE AMBITIOUS MOTHER AND THE OBLIGING CLERGYMAN.

The heavy emphasis on money in the American social scene was criticized not only by European observers, but by many Americans as well. Charles Dana Gibson, whose lovely girls typified the contemporary idea of feminine beauty, had a sharp eye for the foibles of his time. These two drawings are from his book *The Social Ladder*, published in 1902. He does not spare the pen in satirizing the custom of marrying for money, or the social aspirations of the vulgar new rich.

MRS. STEELE POOLE'S HOUSEWARMING.

On this page and the next are paintings by two artists which portray faithfully and charmingly the American young lady of leisure. The picture above, "Tea Leaves," by William M. Paxton, was painted in 1909; the Sargent, on the next page, in 1897; but one must remember that the mood of the eighties and nineties—especially as far as the position and behavior of the well-bred young woman was concerned—lingered on well beyond the turn of the century. One may suppose that the young lady above, idly consulting the tea leaves in her cup, is hoping that they predict a future of married happiness, agreeable social life, money enough for comfort and ease, and a reasonable assurance of the continuation of the status quo.

John Singer Sargent (1856-1925) was a leading portrait painter, and a great favorite in American upper social circles, with good reason, for the brilliance and elegance that characterized his work were very flattering. One of his most delightful portraits is the one above, of Mr. and Mrs. I. N. Phelps Stokes. Despite the picture's air of easy spontaneity, it was a long, careful job, Mrs. Stokes posing twenty-eight times.

In the preceding pages we have moved in rather exalted social circles, for the reason that these circles held what seems to us today a curious fascination for the rest of American society. In reading the general magazines of the end of the nineteenth century, and as late as the early decades of the twentieth, one gets the impression that only the rich and fashionable were worth thinking about. The doings of these happy few were recorded with scrupulous attention. What they wore, how they amused themselves, where they traveled—all their doings were reported in faithful detail, and, one supposes, received by the readers with the same earnest interest. So great was their influence that the manners and customs of the rest of the population who had any claim to polite ways were patterned accordingly, insofar as money permitted. On this page we leave Fifth Avenue and New York and move north into a Maine town to see a group of young people who undoubtedly managed to enjoy life although they lived far from the splendors of a metropolis. They are wearing the approved summer attire for young men and girls toward the end of the century.

Some of the outdoor diversions in which women engaged in the nineties had started a generation or so earlier. Croquet, for example, was played in the sixties; Winslow Homer's painting, above, dates from 1866; and the photograph below shows that archery was popular in Wells College in 1875.

Coaching, particularly in the White Mountains and the Adirondacks, enjoyed a great vogue from the time the New York Coaching Club was formed in 1875. "The Fairman Rogers Four-in-Hand" above was painted by Thomas Eakins in 1879. A less expensive amusement (it cost about $20,000 to buy and operate a coach for a season) was a boat ride up the Hudson River, as pictured in *Harper's Weekly*, September 13, 1890.

The process, begun with the introduction of croquet, of bringing women out of the house to play games and compete in outdoor sports with men was immensely speeded up by the craze for bicycling. Although the bicycle appeared in the mid-seventies, it was then a formidable machine that towered in the air and required something of a gymnast to master it. Women were scared to try it, but when the "safety" bicycle, with its two wheels of equal—and moderate—size and its light pneumatic tires, appeared, women took it up eagerly. All over the country women were soon riding gaily, and although there was considerable debate about the propriety of a divided skirt or bloomers, the New York *Herald* came out boldly and gave a prize for a costume with bloomers (see page 5). Riverside Drive in New York was highly regarded as a good open stretch for bicycling as you will see above in W. T. Smedley's picture.

Reversing the usual procedure, the bicycle was popular with the masses before it won the approval of the socially elect. But when the latter finally succumbed, they did very well for the sport. At the Michaux Club in New York they learned to ride in changing formation and to perform intricate figures to the music of a band. The *Queen of Fashion* heartily applauded bicycling for women, and an article in the June 1896 issue ran in part: "Time was when women stood quietly by and beheld their brothers priding themselves upon their intelligence, ingenuity, and athletic forms, but those days are things of the past and women now share in the many laborious and enjoyable pursuits once denied them. Cycling builds up their feeble frames and infuses into their dull and sordid thoughts prospects of a bright and cheerful world."

Skating had always been popular in the United States, and skating clubs flourished in most cities. The Philadelphia Skating and Humane Society, founded in the late fifties, was pledged "to foster the art of skating and to save life on frozen rivers and lakes," and its members were equipped with coils of rope in case an emergency should arise. The New York Skating Club likewise was prepared to go to the rescue if any of the crowds of skaters in Central Park got into trouble. The roller skate, invented in 1863 by an Englishman, was instantly adopted in Europe, where large rinks were built. In America, the craze reached such proportions that by 1885 more than $20,000,000 had been invested in roller-skating rinks, which were recognized social centers. A. B. Wenzell's drawing above, made in 1900, suggests that although sports clothes were customary for men, women engaged in athletic sports in their ordinary dress.

There are many who believe that tennis was introduced into this country by a woman—Miss Outerbridge had played it in Bermuda and brought the new game back to Staten Island in 1874. Whether the honor belongs to her or to James Dwight of Boston, the game was liked by women from the start. Starting on the Eastern seaboard, it spread westward until, in the eighties, it was a popular social game in polite circles all over the country. Mixed doubles were more stationary than mobile, according to present-day standards, and any stretch of moderately level lawn served as a court. Below you see Miss Anna Sands and Mrs. Barger Wallach on the courts of the Casino at Newport. Dark blue veils were standard summer equipment before suntan was admired.

People weren't so fussy about their tennis costumes, nor so demanding about the condition of the court, when the photograph above was taken. The wobbly lines and patches of grass or weeds were standard conditions in most seaside or mountain resort tennis courts, and most women players stayed modestly near the baseline and didn't go charging up to the net.

Women's golf got off to a rather slow start in the United States. In the last years of the nineteenth century, some golf clubs on the Eastern seaboard rather reluctantly set aside certain afternoons for the benefit of the wives and daughters of their members, but there was no rush to take advantage of this kindness. A few enthusiasts there were, as these pictures show. No one could accuse the sturdy player at the right of lack of energetic determination, and the Wellesley campus in 1900 (below) presented a scene of intense activity that was less alarming than it appears: the students were taking lessons, not playing, and besides, they didn't hit the balls very far. In the July 1894 issue of *The Queen of Fashion*, a writer disagreed with those who said that golf, beyond putting, was not a game for ladies, and remarked that it was not as violent as tennis, which had been accepted. "After all, it is not strength that is required, but knack and neatness." The article ended on a persuasive note: "Golf clothes of the most extraordinary and brilliant nature are already in the hands of the dealers, and golf shoes, a trifle thicker than shooting shoes, are in process of manufacture."

At the Tuxedo Horse Show (above) in about 1909, spectators wore costumes of great elegance. Looking at the tiny purse hanging from the wrist of the woman with the fur, one wonders at the size of handbag the woman of today finds necessary. The Gibson bathing girls below, drawn in 1900, belonged, one imagines, to the spectator class too. There wasn't a bathing cap among them, and the obligatory stockings, though not undecorative on the beach, had a way of coming off in any kind of surf.

"You push the button; we do the rest" was the slogan of the Kodak, introduced by the Eastman Dry Plate and Film Company in the summer of 1888. Transparent flexible film was produced the following year, and the camera craze was launched. The young lady at the right, who is examining her new possession with such satisfaction, is posing against a fine example of the kind of background that was favored by photographers of the nineties. How different is the scene below. Here is no studio background; the earnest photographer is planning to capture a scene of stark reality. Just why she has selected this particular subject we do not know—possibly the horse is an old and beloved friend.

Mr. William K. Vanderbilt, at the left, is at the wheel of his new car, with his first wife (the former Miss Fair) beside him. The car below is a French model. It was once possible to get in and out of a car gracefully.

By the turn of the century the wealthy had a new sport—automobiling. In the August 19, 1899, issue of *Harper's Weekly* one reads: "A ride in an electric cab has ceased to be a novelty, but the amateur conducting of an automobile possesses exhaustless possibilities. In Paris and Newport it has been advanced to the dignity of a sport, and such indeed it is. . . . With the first turn of the wheels, driving an automobile becomes a game between the man and the machine, complicated, it may be, by the presence of other men and other machines."

It was some time before the gasoline-powered automobile gained the ascendancy. At first the electric outnumbered everything else, and there was also the car powered by steam, like the White Steamer shown below. In 1904, when this picture was taken, it was still a highly uncertain undertaking to attempt to drive any distance in a car. Dusty roads and the lack of windshields necessitated a costume something like the one on the model at the right. *Harper's Weekly* for July 22, 1899, carries an account of the remarkable achievement of Alexander Winton, who left Cleveland on Monday, May 22, and arrived at City Hall, New York, on Friday, May 26, having covered nearly 708 miles, "one of the longest [runs] on record," with a running time of 47 hours and 34 minutes at an average speed of 15 miles per hour. "The only accident of importance was at Fairport, N. Y., where the carriage, while running at a speed of 25 miles per hour, was ditched, and had its front running gear badly smashed up. Luckily, Mr. Winton and his companion escaped serious injury."

Mindful of the rigors of touring, the makers of the Marmon car in 1907 advertised their product as follows: "Do you want a car in which a woman can tour without fear of exhaustion and without injury to her health? The Marmon is the only car that fully satisfies this requirement."

As late as 1910, there were many conservatives who looked askance at a woman driving a car. It was considered just a trifle fast. Miss Chrystal Herne, at the right, was an actress, and was therefore perhaps more daring than the purely domestic woman might be. As late as 1920 an item in the *Ladies' Home Journal* suggested that women drivers were not entirely taken for granted. It said: "No one is more graceful or attractive to watch than a woman who has acquired 'form' in driving an automobile. Gliding in and out through traffic, having absolute control over every movement of her car, she seems almost a part of the machine itself." The young lady above is at the wheel of a Stutz. Some readers will remember when the Stutz Bearcat was the heart's desire of the younger set.

That Europe was the real home of culture was the pious belief of most educated Americans in the late nineteenth and early twentieth centuries, and a trip abroad was a certain mark of a cultivated American. An article in the July 16, 1892, issue of *Harper's Weekly* comments on the great liners that made the passage in only six days, and says, "The American's dream of happiness is going abroad; and the better American he is, the more he longs for a trip to the Old World. . . . Today it is no exaggeration to say that one's education can hardly be called complete without a European excursion as a final touch to the home polish." The picture above, drawn by C. S. Reinhart for *Harper's Weekly* for March 1, 1890, shows American visitors to Paris inspecting the "Venus of Milo" in the Louvre.

The elongated elegance and dignified bearing of Consuelo Vanderbilt, daughter of Mr. and Mrs. W. K. Vanderbilt, were well suited to the court dress of a duchess. The portrait of her shown above was taken when she was the Duchess of Marlborough.

Lovely Jennie Jerome, the daughter of a New York banker, married Lord Randolph Churchill in the seventies and started a trend of international marriages which reached such proportions that the term "Dollar Princesses" was coined to describe many American girls who were happy to bring papa's millions to the rescue of ancient but financially embarrassed European estates. A list of fifty-seven alliances between American women and foreign noblemen was published in *McCall's* for November 1903, including such resplendent ones as these: Lord Curzon and Miss Mary Leiter, Marquis de Talleyrand-Perigord and Miss Curtis, Count de Castellane and Miss Anna Gould, Duc de la Rochefoucauld and Miss Mattie Mitchell, Earl of Orford and Miss Louise Corbin. When Miss May Goelet became the Duchess of Roxburghe in November 1903 the crowds outside St. Thomas's Church (below) showed with what keen interest New Yorkers regarded the event. The Duchess is pictured at the right. One doubts if the same enthusiasm animated the unmarried countrywomen of these foreign bridegrooms, and indeed the May 17, 1913, issue of *Harper's Weekly* carried a reply to an English writer, Rita, who had been saying some pretty sharp things about American women. Rita was quoted as having declared that the American had debased London society with "her slang, her free and easy manners, her vulgar modes of eating and drinking and speaking."

LAND, HO!—SCENE ON BOARD AN EMIGRANT SHIP.

While Americans of the leisure class were crossing the Atlantic to enjoy the scenic beauties and art treasures of the Old World, Europeans of a quite different status were making the journey westward to seek their fortunes in the new country. Starvation in Ireland, political discontent in Germany, and appalling poverty plus miserable working conditions throughout Europe drove thousands each year to the land where there was a warm welcome for cheap labor couched in the high-sounding phrase: "Asylum for the Oppressed of Every Land." The scene above, portraying the sighting of land aboard an emigrant ship, appeared in *Harper's Weekly* for June 3, 1871. The tide continued in mounting numbers, and through the first decade of this century immigrants were coming at the rate of close to a million a year. The gates were partly closed by quota laws beginning in 1921, and further narrowed by immigration policy in the nineteen-thirties.

The picture below of a New York sweat shop shows the kind of "asylum" that many of the immigrants found waiting for them in the New World. An indignant article in *Harper's Weekly* for April 26, 1890, says: "Coming from the grinding conditions of labor in the Old World . . . the toiler is at once confronted with the drawbacks of an overcrowded community. . . . He falls into the hands of the 'sweater' and thenceforward, if his life is better than it was in Poland or Hungary—and it is—it is solely because of the larger liberty he has, and because of that bow of promise that is ever before him, and that will, so long as he lives, remain in the distance like an actual rainbow." The women as well as the men were exploited shamelessly, five cents an hour for unremitting toil was about what the newly arrived worker could expect, and the majority of women who did not go into domestic service found themselves victims of the ugly practices that formerly existed in the garment industry: either helping their husbands in their miserable homes or submitting to the deplorable conditions of overcrowded, evil-smelling lofts. The article continues: "This creature [the 'sweater'] is not a toiler, not a merchant, not a producer, not even a dealer in anything but human endurance. He is a contractor, and the name 'sweater' by which he is commonly called is indicative of the character of his employment. . . . To him it matters little how small the price of the work is if he can secure enough of it, for he looks out for his own pay first, and pays the workmen whom he employs whatever is left. He serves no purpose whatever in the economy of civilization beyond the mere convenience of the manufacturer."

The searing photographs on this page and the one opposite were taken in New York by Jacob Riis and are among the illustrations in his famous books, *The Battle With The Slums* (1902) and *How The Other Half Lives* (1892). The picture at the left was made in the home of an Italian rag-picker on Jersey Street. The miserable sheds around the yard below—also in Jersey Street—were inhabited by Italians who paid $1 a week for the privilege of subsisting in them. In *The Battle With The Slums* Riis wrote, "Jersey Street, a short block between Mulberry and Crosby Streets, to which no Whitechapel slum could hold a candle, became a factory street. No one lives there now. The last who did was murdered by the gang that grew as naturally out of its wickedness as a toadstool grows on a rotten log."

The photograph at the right shows old Mrs. Benoit in her attic on Hudson Street. Presumably there is a small space in which she could stand upright. The scene below shows the 47th Street Police Station, where people who had nowhere else to go could spend the night. Riis's comment was: "The police station lodging rooms . . . were not to be dignified by the term. These vile dens, in which the homeless of our great city were herded, without pretence of bed, of bath, of food, on rude planks, were the most pernicious parody on municipal charity, I verily believe, that any civilized community had ever devised." These pictures were made in New York, but slum conditions in other American cities were equally shameful.

The Triangle Waist Company had little to recommend it as a place to work. Isaac Harris and Max Blanck, the owners, paid their employees on a piece-work basis—and kept the rate as low as possible. Working hours were from 7:30 in the morning to 6 in the evening, six days a week. An exceptionally rapid girl who worked overtime evenings and Sundays could make as much as $18 a week, but many only got $6 to $8. Working conditions in the old Asch Building on Washington Square (New York) were about as bad as could be. Five hundred girls and fifty men worked on the 8th, 9th, and 10th floors—at least 100 feet above the street—and they were so overcrowded that the chairs were dovetailed.

The workers had another grievance besides discomfort in the spring of 1911. Styles had changed, shirtwaists were more elaborate, and, accordingly, took longer to make, but the girls were still paid for the number they finished. Harris and Blanck were having their troubles too. They had suffered considerably in the recent shirtwaist strike. It had started in one of their factories, and their workers had been the last to return. One good thing they did have: fire insurance on the Asch Building amounting to $199,750.

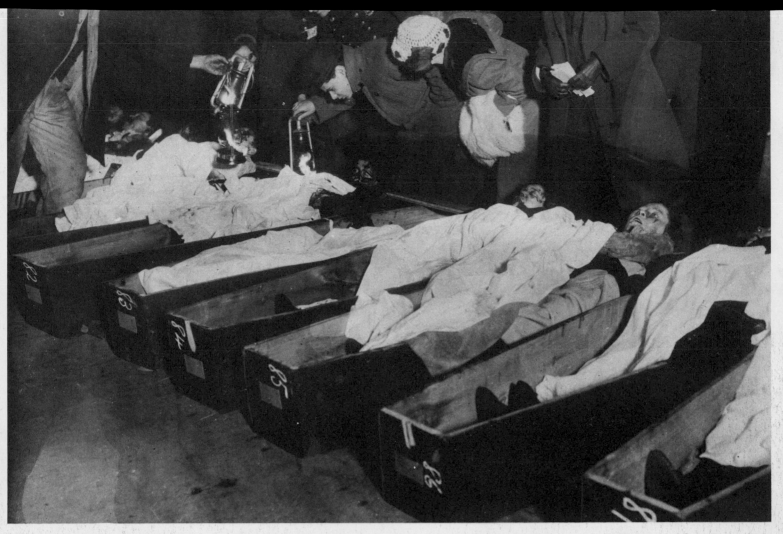

It seems incredible that the owners could have got any fire insurance at all on the Asch Building under the circumstances: beneath every sewing machine the floor was soaked with oil and two barrels of oil stood on the 8th and the 9th floors; bins beneath the cutters' tables were filled with scraps; oil-soaked rags and lint were everywhere, and the shelves and baskets were full of inflammable muslin. There was one narrow door on each floor, usually kept locked for fear the girls would steal something. Disaster struck in the afternoon of April 20, 1911, when fire broke out and raged through the three floors, killing at least 145 girls. Harris and Blanck were indicted for manslaughter, but were acquitted.

The pictures on these two pages show, opposite, above, the twisted, inadequate fire escapes, and below that, the pitiful bodies of a few of the girls who had jumped. In the photograph above, the harrowing business of identifying the victims at the Morgue is going on, while at the right you see relatives leaving the Morgue after identifying the dead. If you wonder at the severity of some of the reformers shown in the following pages, remember such episodes as the Triangle fire.

FIRST FEMINISTS

Although the Victorian ideal of the sheltered lady was generally accepted in 19th-century America as representing the most enviable status a woman could have, there was a growing revolt against this concept of bourgeois respectability by strong-minded individual women. The first public declaration of this revolt was made in July 1848 at Seneca Falls, New York, when Lucretia Mott, Quaker, Abolitionist, and temperance worker, with Elizabeth Cady Stanton (another reformer of vigorous intelligence) and a few others organized the first Woman's Rights meeting. The stamp above commemorates the 100th anniversary of that memorable event, with portraits of Mrs. Mott, Mrs. Stanton, and Carrie Chapman Catt, who was chosen by Susan B. Anthony in 1900 to succeed her as president of the National Woman Suffrage Association. Mrs. Catt also helped organize the International Suffrage Alliance and served as its president from 1904 to 1923, and was the founder of the League of Women Voters.

From the age of seventeen, when she was a teacher in rural New York, Susan B. Anthony agitated for woman's rights; and from 1851, when she met Mrs. Stanton at a temperance meeting, the two worked closely together for universal suffrage. Miss Anthony was the founder and first president of the National Woman Suffrage Association. She is shown at the left.

Later in time than the first pioneers was Charlotte Perkins Gilman (left, below), a lecturer and writer in the cause of labor and in the feminist movement. In her book, *Woman and Economics* (1898), she made a strong plea for economic independence for women. Her humorous and nimble mind won many converts who might have resisted the moralizing of other reformers.

WOMAN'S WORK

Despite Mrs. Gilman's thesis that only by complete economic independence from "the nearest male relative by birth or marriage" could women throw off the fetters of tradition, there weren't very many avenues open to them for gainful employment—with society's approval —until as late as World War I. Teaching was the classic occupation for women, but although some illustrious names of the last century come to mind at once, like those of Maria Mitchell, teacher of astronomy at Vassar, Emma Willard, founder of the Troy Female Seminary, and Alice Freeman Palmer, president of Wellesley, the overwhelming majority taught in elementary schools and achieved small reputation outside of their own classrooms. The painting above, "The Country School," by Edward L. Henry (1890), gives a fairly grim idea of the profession. The young teachers at the right, however, have not been completely crushed by outrageous fortune. This merry photograph was taken in 1893 in Moriah, New York.

Surely one of the most remarkable teachers of all time was Anne Mansfield Sullivan. The daughter of poor Irish immigrants, she was placed in an almshouse as a child when her mother died and her father disappeared. Her eyes had been badly affected by an early infection, and when this was discovered (in the course of an investigation of the wretched conditions of the almshouse) she was permitted to go to Perkins Institute for the Blind. She was then fourteen. At the Institute she learned a manual language, and when a Captain Keller of Tuscumbia, Alabama, applied there in 1887 for someone to be a teacher for his seven-year-old daughter, Helen, who was deaf and blind as a result of illness when she was nineteen months old, Anne Sullivan undertook the apparently hopeless assignment. Helen Keller graduated *cum laude* from Radcliffe at twenty-four. This charming photograph of the two reveals something of the tender bond between them, a bond that proved to be lifelong.

JULIA WARD HOWE

LAURA E. RICHARDS

MARGARET DELAND

MARY JOHNSTON

FANNIE M. FARMER

It is my intention, in this book, to compare women and men as little as possible. I don't think you can measure their various accomplishments by the same yardstick. However, when one comes upon a field where the performance of women may be justly compared with that of men, it is interesting to see the results. By "justly" I mean that no artificial or extraneous conditions enter into the picture. This is particularly true in the field of writing. Granted that some women formerly thought it advisable to use a masculine nom de plume for purposes of modesty or whatever, there is no real sex discrimination in training, wages, or working conditions in the writing of books. It may be significant that the best-selling books in the United States between 1852 and 1861 were divided equally between the sexes—twelve authors were women, twelve were men. (The titles included *Uncle Tom's Cabin*; *Walden*; *John Halifax, Gentleman*; *A Tale of Two Cities*; and *East Lynne*.)

EDITH WHARTON

It would be impossible to do more than suggest in this type of book the variety and scope of the women writers of this country. On this page you see six of the many feminine authors who contributed to American letters in the late nineteenth and early twentieth centuries. Julia Ward Howe, author of "The Battle Hymn of the Republic," was the first woman to be elected to the American Academy of Arts and Sciences; Laura E. Richards, her daughter, wrote among other charming books *Captain January*; Margaret Deland, whose *John Ward, Preacher* was a best seller of 1888, was still producing in the mid-twenties; Mary Johnston's historical novels were immensely popular at the turn of the century. Her *To Have and to Hold* came out in 1900, followed two years later by *Audrey*; Edith Wharton startled her fashionable friends in 1905 by her satire of them, *The House of Mirth,* and produced a smashing hit in 1921 with *The Age of Innocence*; and in another area entirely was Fannie Merritt Farmer, whose *Boston Cooking-School Cook Book*, published in 1896, has sold over two million copies.

PRIESTESSES OF PASSION

Poems of Passion by Ella Wheeler Wilcox, a thumping success and big best seller of 1883, was bad poetry by any standards. One reviewer said that the book had more passion in the title than anywhere else and that it "could not disturb the morals of a lady-bug." The author is shown here twice: as a young lady between the parted portieres, and in later years with a fine cat sharing her desk. But if Poems of Passion belied its name, Elinor Glyn's Three Weeks gave the purchasers their money's worth of sex. (Evidently the readers' boiling point was considerably lower in 1907 than it is today.) This tale of a three-weeks' illicit honeymoon (largely spent on a tiger-skin rug) of a queen and an Adonis of an Englishman was a run-away best seller and a storm center of controversy. The Baltimore Sun declared it to be "an example of the most brilliant twentieth century fiction." The St. Paul Pioneer Press considered it "fit only for the garbage pail." Mrs. Glyn is shown above at the left.

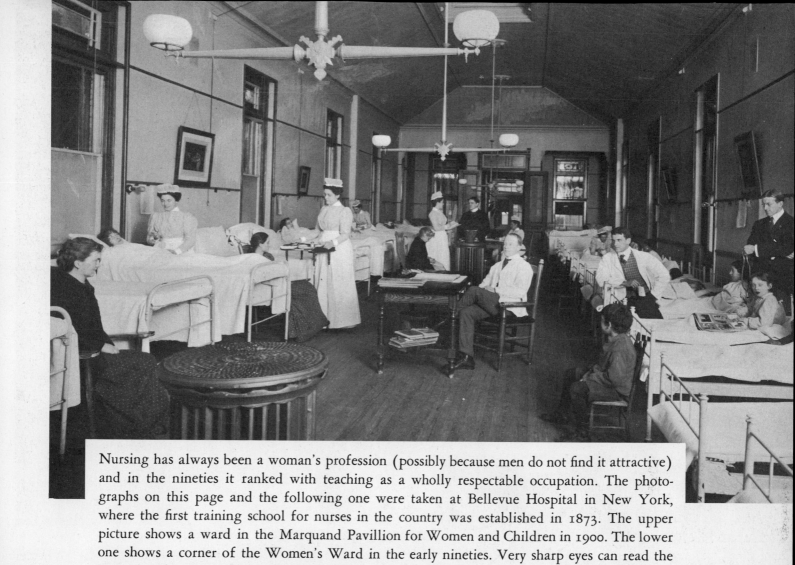

Nursing has always been a woman's profession (possibly because men do not find it attractive) and in the nineties it ranked with teaching as a wholly respectable occupation. The photographs on this page and the following one were taken at Bellevue Hospital in New York, where the first training school for nurses in the country was established in 1873. The upper picture shows a ward in the Marquand Pavillion for Women and Children in 1900. The lower one shows a corner of the Women's Ward in the early nineties. Very sharp eyes can read the motto on the wall, which offers the patients pretty cold comfort. It says, "No Pain, no Palm; no Thorn, no Throne; no Cross, no Crown."

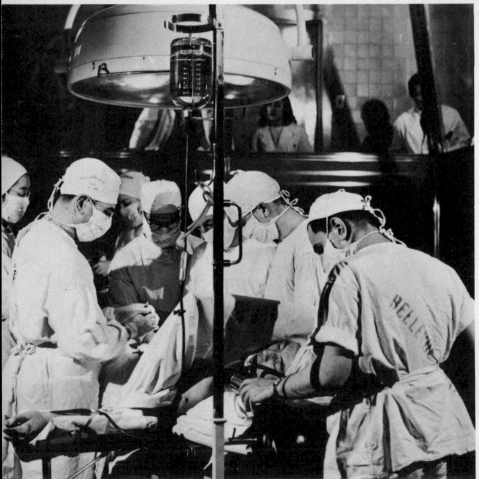

Both photographs on this page show operations being performed at Bellevue, the upper one, some time in the nineties, the lower, as of today. Do not be misled by the apparent casual informality of the earlier scene. The doctors and nurses were quite as serious and as concentrated as now, although antiseptic and prophylactic standards were not so high, and doctors wore white coats, if at all, not for the sake of the patient, but to protect their own clothes.

Frances Eaton Pope, writing in 1898, advised girls that it took great physical strength to be a nurse, and added, "The leaving home is a great question to be weighed. It may mean a complete change in your life, and is something which you only can decide—and this decision should be made carefully and prayerfully." In 1880 there were 157 graduate nurses in the country; there were 3,500 in 1900; 15,000 in 1920, and over 25,000 in 1930; while the number of nursing schools had grown during the same fifty years from 15 to 1,900.

MODJESKA

MAUDE ADAMS

The theatre, like literature, has long provided an opportunity for women of talent to distinguish themselves, and theatrical history is studded with the names of brilliant feminine stars. Although the profession as a whole was eyed askance by the ultra respectable, well into the nineteen hundreds, there have always been actresses of unimpeachable personal dignity. A few of these Caesar's wives are here shown: Modjeska, brightest ornament of the '80's and '90's, Maude Adams in *The Little Minister* (1897), the young Julia Marlowe as Juliet (late nineties), and the lovely Mary Anderson, pride of Louisville and London's darling.

JULIA MARLOWE

MARY ANDERSON

Ethel Barrymore (signature)

Ethel Barrymore, daughter of Maurice and Georgie Barrymore and sister of Lionel and John, came from probably the most noted American family of actors. After playing minor parts in her uncle John Drew's company, she emerged as a Frohman star in 1901, playing the lead in Clyde Fitch's *Captain Jinks of the Horse Marines.* You see her in this part at the left, and mighty captivating she is too.

Mrs. Leslie Carter was a pupil of Frohman's famous rival, David Belasco. She was no child of the theatre, but a young society woman from Chicago who had suffered unpleasant publicity because of a divorce. Under Belasco's direction she became a famous star, first in 1895 in *The Heart of Maryland* (also by Clyde Fitch), and then in 1899 in *Zaza*, in which she is shown below. William Winter, the dramatic critic, disapproved highly of plays about immoral women, but conceded that Mrs. Carter's performance was "much admired. . . . It was the utter reckless abandon, the uncontrolled physical and vocal vehemence, the virago-like intensity of her abuse of her lover, which, communicating themselves to the nerves of her auditors and overwhelming them by violence, gained the actress her success in the part."

Lillian Russell, shown at the right in full panoply, at Proctor's in the early twentieth century, is wearing a gown of Irish lace and an assortment of very fine feathers. She was famous for her blond and opulent beauty, her magnificence in dress, and her habit of marrying often. She also sang in light opera, making her debut in *Pinafore* in the late seventies, when she was eighteen. She was a brilliant figure in the café life and sporting circles of her time, and was often seen on the arm of Diamond Jim Brady. She was ignored by New York's "Four Hundred," but as the wife of her fourth husband, Alexander P. Moore, Ambassador to Spain, she achieved great popularity in that stronghold of punctilio, the Spanish court.

Temptation is represented below in the scene from *Mlle Fifi*, in which Aubrey Boucicault as the Vicomte de Puissac and Louise Baudet, of the Folies-Bergère, dally in a Turkish corner whose proportions are anything but cosy. A few moments later, Mlle Fifi will shamelessly twitch her skirts and reveal her legs—encased in black tights.

Nan Patterson (left) was a member of the original double sextet of the famous *Floradora,* which was produced in 1900, ran 547 performances in New York, and played in nearly every city in the United States. On June 4, 1904, she was riding in a hansom cab in New York with one Frank Thomas Young, known as "Caesar" (because his profile closely resembled that of the great Roman), a wealthy bookmaker. They were on their way to the White Star docks, where Mrs. Young was waiting, in anticipation of a European voyage. The cabby heard a shot, and discovered Mr. Young dying of a pistol wound. Miss Patterson was arrested, spent eleven months in prison, stood trial for her life three times, and finally was acquitted.

The Miller Sisters (right) show what wholesome girls could succeed in vaudeville. The chorus of *Twiddle Twaddle* (below), led by the stalwart girl in modified military costume, are introducing a roguish device that later became extremely popular. You will see that in the center of their ermine muffs there is a bit of looking glass. The light from the footlights was reflected in these and turned in the faces of promising gentlemen of the audience to their embarrassment or delight.

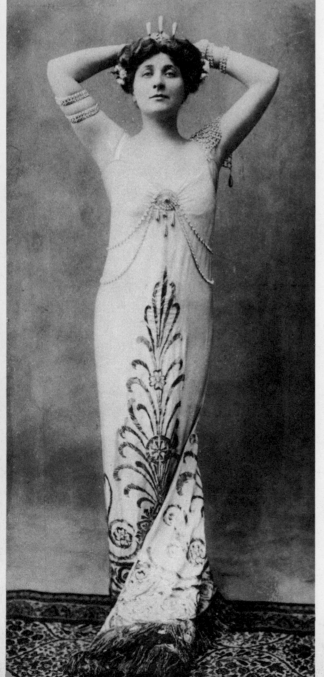

Nowhere was American reverence for European supremacy in the arts more clearly demonstrated than in the opera. It was popularly believed that of course European artists sang better, and those American stars who achieved the top rank did not venture to sing in this country until they had studied in Europe and made a successful debut abroad. Here are three outstanding American opera singers. Emma Eames (left, above) had beauty and versatility (she was equally at home in the roles of Bruennehilde and Marguerite) and retired when her voice was still at its peak. Mary Garden (left, below) was an overnight sensation in 1900 when she was called on suddenly to sing *Louise* at the Paris Opera. She is here shown as Thais, one of her most sensational parts. When Geraldine Farrar (above, as Juliet), then a member of the Berlin opera, first sang in Paris on May 20, 1905, a critic cabled, "Her voice is pure and clear, her methods are simple, and, what is rare, she can act." In the curious photograph below, she and her husband, Lou Tellegen, enjoy a quiet evening at home. The tiger-skin rug gives a *Three Weeks* touch.

We have already remarked on the socially acceptable occupations for women in the nineteenth century and the early decades of the twentieth—teaching and nursing (and badly paid they were, according to any standards)—and have suggested the outstanding performance of gifted women as writers, actresses, and singers (whose financial rewards were often handsome indeed). There were thousands of others, however, who had no particular talent and couldn't afford to worry about social status when it came to making a living. Many of these women were in factories, and although the hours were long (the twelve-hour day was not unusual) and they were paid only about one-third as much as men for the same work, conditions were not always as horrendous as those in the garment industry in New York. The scene above, for example, taken in the box department of the Eastman Kodak Company in Rochester in 1906, suggests an intelligent and humane management; and the photograph below, showing the start of a 50-yard dash at a picnic of the Packard Motor Car Company in August 1911, reveals earnest effort on the part of all concerned.

The acceptance of the typewriter opened a new world to the American working woman—and how she conquered it! In 1870, there were only seven women stenographers in the country. By 1900, there were 200,000, and by 1930 there were two million. And as the number of women soared, the number of men dwindled. In 1910, men held 1/6 of the stenographic and typing jobs; by 1930, only 1/25.

In 1881 Remington sold 1200 machines, and their first catalogue of typewriters offers the following service: "Stenographers can come to our office and dictate to operators from their shorthand notes and thus save the labor of transcription." The scene below shows the main office of the Eastman Kodak Company in the nineties. You will observe the roll-top desks, the formality of the men's attire, and the standard (and most decorous) dress that was the correct uniform for the business girl of the time.

The drawing above was made from a photograph taken in 1872. It shows the daughter of Christopher Sholes, inventor of the first practical typewriter, operating one of her father's machines. This early model bears a strong resemblance to a sewing machine, with its foot pedal which returned the carriage.

"The ambition of every girl who goes into business as a stenographer—provided she has a goal and does not merely regard her position as a means of filling the interim between school and matrimony—is to become a private secretary. Certainly the ambition is a laudable one for, short of actual executive work, it is about the most agreeable and lucrative kind of position one can hold. . . ." So wrote Helen B. Gladwyn in an article in *The Ladies' Home Journal* for September 1916. And another article of about the same time defined as necessary for a good secretary "that quality that helps one to serve quietly and happily without recognition, content to understand the social value of the task in question." This office scene shows a private secretary of the nineties, quietly and happily serving.

Although the office above is a far cry from the luxurious suites of many top executives of today (particularly as shown in the movies), this private office of Charles M. Schwab in 1910 indicates a trend away from the austerity of an earlier time. Besides, Mr. Schwab had one convenience that is missing from modern offices—a highly polished brass spittoon.

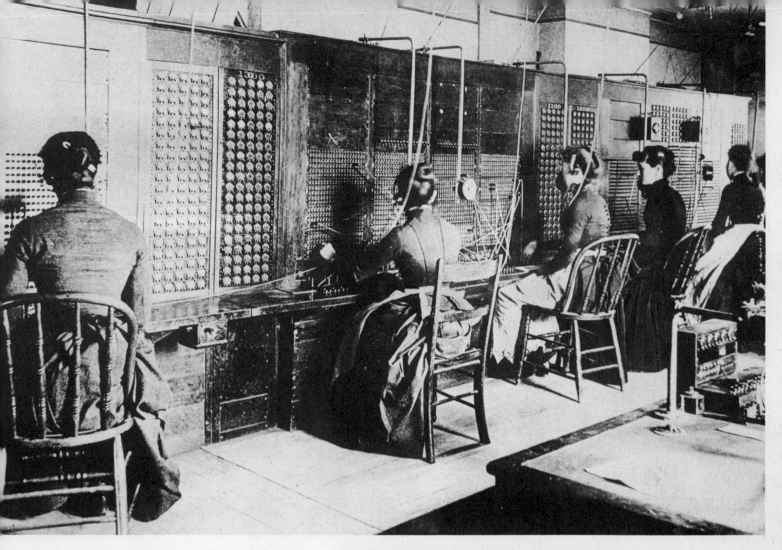

From the beginning, women have been particularly adept as telephone operators. Oddly enough, although the first telephones were installed in the White House in 1878, it was not until Louise Hachmeister was brought there in 1933 that a woman was added to the switchboard staff. The theory was that women couldn't keep secrets. Miss Hachmeister shot that theory into small bits, and it wasn't long before she and five women assistants manned the White House telephone switchboard.

The upper photograph shows the Milwaukee switchboard in 1883 and the lower one is of the first emergency board set up in downtown San Francisco after the, shall we say, fire of April 1906. Although the phrase "The Voice With a Smile" was not coined until 1912, the New York Telephone Company had an operators' school as early as 1902, headed by Miss Katherine M. Schmitt (who had been an operator since 1882 and retired in 1929), where the girls were taught clear speech, politeness, and iron control of tempers under all circumstances.

Even in the late nineties, the telephone was considered an instrument for business, few people had them in their homes, and to deliver an invitation by telephone was generally regarded as extremely bad form.

Miss Dorothy Stickney, as Mrs. Day in the long-lived play, "Life With Father," recreated with consummate charm the sheltered lady of tradition. It is a mistake to confuse leisure with idleness. The lady of leisure seldom sat with folded hands. She had certain accomplishments which she practiced—playing a musical instrument, painting water colors, or china-painting—and various hand crafts. Often the products of her hand were so beautifully made that they could be classed as works of art. Exquisite needlework—sewing or embroidery —she did in surprising volume, considering how long it took. It is possibly significant that as time went on and the position of housekeeper began to lose prestige, these home crafts degenerated. In the early nineteen hundreds such fads as pyrography (burnt leather or wood), raffia work, and Indian bead work were taken up in place of the time-consuming silk embroidery or making of monograms. There was no slackening of interest in the well set table, however. A menu for Christmas dinner in *McCall's* for December 1903 suggests: cream of tomato soup, roast goose, turkey, turnips, mashed potatoes, chicken pudding, ham, apple sauce, cranberry sauce, squash, oyster plant, celery salad, plum pudding, mince pie, café parfait, velvet cream, macaroons, and coffee.

OCCUPATION: HOUSEWIFE

The lady of the house in America's upper middle class in the Grant-Cleveland era was an executive with a fairly complex organization to handle. Sheltered she might be, but her shelter took a good deal of looking after. If her husband was even moderately wealthy ("comfortably well off" was the term) she had two or three servants indoors and a man who took care of the furnace and was on call for such jobs as washing the windows, polishing the brass, shoveling the snow, etc. There was a nurse for the children, a coachman if the family had horses, a gardener if the grounds warranted. A laundress came weekly—or sent her children to collect and deliver the family laundry. A seamstress spent two weeks in the house spring and autumn (if there was no sewing-room, a spare bedroom was put to this use). The kitchen was a beehive of industry all day long. Canned food, baker's bread, "bought" ice-cream were frowned on. Nice people ate homemade food. Preserves and pickles and jellies were made at home from family recipes. Only imported olive oil was suitable for salad dressings; oleomargarine was beneath contempt; and it was a very black mark against you if you were suspected of using cooking butter or cooking sherry. Spring and fall housecleaning were weeks of feverish activity, with extra hands in to wash the paint, take up the carpets, put down the matting (or vice versa). And all of these operations the lady of the house supervised with an eagle eye. Is was a real compliment to be called a good housekeeper.

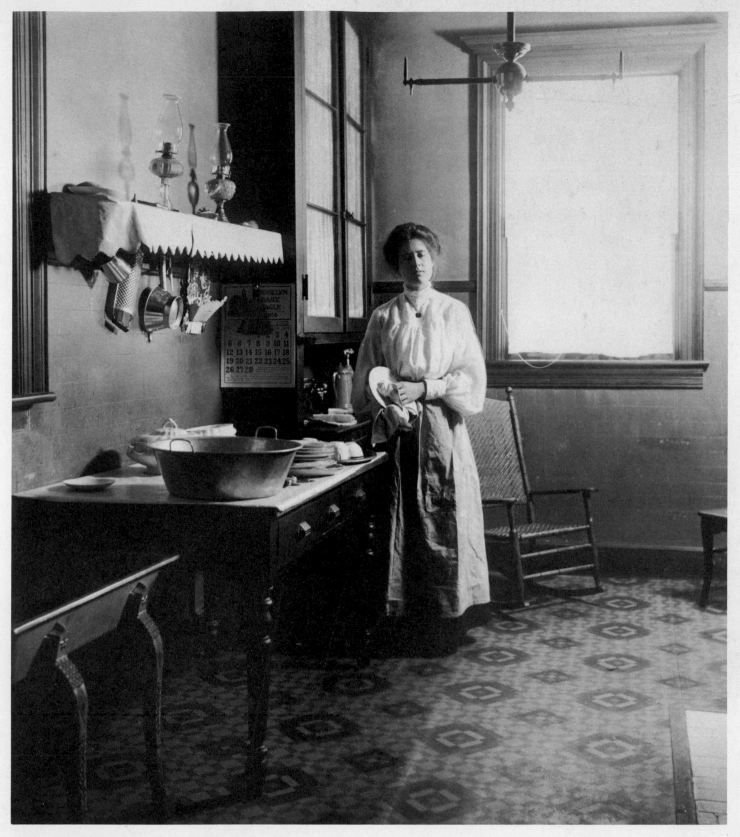

The good old days may indeed have been good—for a very small minority of the population. The comfort of the Victorian household we've been discussing rested solidly upon the labor of the domestic servants, and while there were undoubtedly many kind and conscientious mistresses and contented employees, there were also thousands of cases where the servants had a very thin time. Especially was this true of the maid-of-all-work. The cheerless scene above shows a typical kitchen of 1905. Hours were long, tasks were endless, pay was meager. Moreover, the social status of the servant was at the very bottom of the scale. One reads with dismay the advice on "How to Keep Good Servants" in the May 1895 issue of the *Queen of Fashion*. The implications back of the following points are clear—and embarrassing: Give as good wages as you can, and pay regularly or explain why you must ask her to wait. Give her a pleasant room and time to keep it tidy. Don't let the children be disrespectful or make unnecessary work. Don't reprimand her before the children or strangers. Always say "please" and "thank you" when you ask her to do anything for you, and insist that the children do the same. Do not scold, blame, or find fault more than you can possibly help.

When little Phoebe Annie Oakley Mozee was nine years old, she could shoot the head off a running quail; this ability came in very handy in a household that couldn't afford butcher shops. In 1875, when she was fifteen, she went to Cincinnati to take part in a shooting match, and there met the dashing Frank Butler whom she married a little more than a year later. Annie Oakley toured with her husband for years in Buffalo Bill's Wild West Show and delighted audiences in America and Europe with her prodigious feats. She could split a playing card edgewise, knock the ash from Butler's cigarette, and one of her prettiest tricks was shooting the heart out of the ace of hearts with 25 shots at 25 yards—in 27 seconds. She is shown, above, as a girl, and below, in later years. Beginning in May 1946, theatre-goers in New York enjoyed the vigorous reincarnation of Annie Oakley as played by Ethel Merman (right) in *Annie Get Your Gun*, which was destined for a run of almost three years.

COMPANION AND RIVAL OF MAN

We have already mentioned, on page 36, a few of the early pioneers for women's rights who were the complete antithesis of the sheltered lady. Still another concept was growing in the United States in the early decades of the twentieth century: woman was to be a companion and rival of man. This role was not so clearly defined as that of the sheltered lady or the strict feminist. The women who played it ranged from the wholesome outdoor girls, the good companions, who could hold their own with men in sports and games, to the single-minded and determined few who made their way in a man's world, asking no quarter, and turning in performances that were outstanding regardless of the sex of the performer. As a rule they were less concerned with women's rights in general than with their own rights as individuals, and they usually lacked the hostility to men that characterized many of the early reformers.

The roots of this concept go far back in American life. The pioneer woman was perforce a companion to the pioneer man and shared to the limit of her physical strength (sometimes beyond it) the strenuous effort of daily life. On this page and the next are a few picturesque characters from the old West who, in various ways, demonstrated rugged individualism.

Recent students of the American frontier have been pretty hard on Martha Jane (Canary) Burke, popularly known as Calamity Jane, but there was a time when her reputation for bravery, for skill with firearms, and for horsemanship shone brightly. It is now believed that she excelled chiefly in the arts of story-telling and drinking, and that her account of her activities as one of Custer's scouts was purely her own invention. She is shown above in the masculine clothes which she often wore and in the other photograph she and one of her many gentlemen friends have exchanged hats to make it funnier. Mrs. Nathaniel Collins, at the left, known as "The Cattle Queen of Montana," was something else again. Her own account of her early life occasionally strains the reader's credulity, so full is it of encounters with mountain lions at a tender age, her capture by Indians, and a narrow escape from being burned at the stake. However, it is true that she did amass a sizable fortune in stock-raising and became a substantial member of her community. A Montana newspaper wrote of her, "Personally, Mrs. Collins is a charming lady. There is nothing masculine in her appearance or conversation. . . . Socially she is very highly esteemed by all who know her, and in the financial and business centers she commands universal admiration for her thorough knowledge on every subject of her affairs."

On April 22, 1889, when Oklahoma was opened to white settlers, some 50,000 homesteaders, held in check by troops, were waiting on the border. At noon the signal was given and a mad stampede followed. In the photograph at the right you see women as well as men ready and waiting to join in the rush for the best sites.

The Harvey Girls made their way in a man's world in an experiment conducted by Fred Harvey, with his string of restaurants operating along the Santa Fe Railroad. He decided that good food and decorous service would pay out in a region where such things were unheard of. He was right. By 1893 he had control of all the hotels and restaurants on the Santa Fe system, and was advertising in newspapers all over the East and Middle West for "Young women of good character, attractive and intelligent, 18 to 30." The good characters were carefully guarded by a matron who watched over her charges with an eagle eye. The girls lived in dormitories, and had to be in by ten o'clock. However, the matrimonial opportunities in a womanless country were so great that it is estimated that about 5,000 of these famous waitresses married men they met first in the dining rooms or at the lunch counters. Mr. Harvey was a stickler for form, refusing, for one thing, to serve customers without coats. Only in Santa Fe did he relax this rule in acknowledgment of the bohemian ways of the artists and writers who congregated there. Once in Las Vegas a group of cowhands rode into the dining room, shot the necks off a few bottles, and made their demands in anything but polite terms. James Marshall, in his book *Santa Fe*, describes the scene: "Mr. Harvey, who was present, maintained his dapper serenity, stepped forward and raised a white hand. 'Gentlemen,' he said, 'ladies dine here. No swearing or foul language is permitted. You must leave quietly at once.' The cowhands, shamed, walked their horses out of the room, being careful that the screen door did not slam. . . ."

The Harvey girl at the right is a comparatively modern version, dating from the nineteen-twenties; but Nelly Bly, above, appears in the costume in which she circled the globe between November 14, 1889, and January 25, 1890, following the path of Phileas Fogg, hero of Jules Verne's novel, *Around the World in Eighty Days*, that appeared in 1872. Nelly Bly was a newspaper woman, working for the New York *World*, when she made her epochal journey.

Three trail-blazers are here shown: Margaret Sanger, Ida M. Tarbell, and Hetty Green. Miss Sanger (above), despite her delicate air, had the fortitude to face savage public denunciation and a term in prison for her principles. As a district nurse in the slums of New York she had been impressed with the desperate financial pressures that large families exerted upon the poor. In 1914 she brought out the first issue of *The Woman Rebel*. It was banned from the mails and she was sentenced to prison. She continued the crusade, and by 1923 had won a moral and practical victory in the opening, in New York City, of the first permanent birth control clinic.

In 1894, S. S. McClure offered Ida Minerva Tarbell an editorial position on *McClure's*, with a salary of $40 a week. Miss Tarbell was an experienced writer with a sound reputation, but she had never expected to earn as much money as that. Her *History of the Standard Oil Company*, which began in *McClure's* in 1902, is a classic of its kind. Her careful scholarship, meticulous documentation, and clear-eyed judgment bore out her middle name and set the pattern for the "literature of exposure," in which she was followed by Lincoln Steffens, with *The Shame of the Cities*, by Ray Stannard Baker, with his article on "Railroads on Trial," and later by many sensationalists whom Theodore Roosevelt called "muckrakers."

Hetty Green (1835-1916), many years older than either Miss Sanger or Miss Tarbell, lacked their high moral purpose. She was out to make money, and so successful was she at this supposedly masculine occupation that she increased, by shrewd manipulation, the fortune left her by her father to the staggering sum of a hundred million dollars, and became known as the greatest woman financier in the world. She is shown at the right.

Eleanora Sears was—and is—the archetype of the "outdoor girl." A proper Bostonian by birth, she grew up in a tradition of physical exercise, but carried it to a point that few women (or men, for that matter) have ever approached. She fenced, rode, shot, played tennis, squash, baseball, hockey, and polo, and even organized a football team on which she played fullback. She drove racing cars and motor boats. She was an early woman motorist (she is shown at the left above in her electric in 1905) and was the first Boston woman to fly solo. That was in 1910. Despite her somewhat forbidding expression in the photograph above, Miss Sears was no man-hater. In the nineteen-hundreds when she was an outstanding beauty (she is still extremely handsome) she was immensely popular with men, and was many times reported to be engaged. Her comment on the general entrance of women into the field of sports, a movement in which she was a natural leader, was that it took place in "an era of enlightenment, of sense, of good fellowship."

The photograph at the left shows Miss Sears ("Eleo" to her friends) playing tennis in 1922. With Hazel V. Hotchkiss (who was later Mrs. G. W. Wightman) she won the national women's doubles championship in 1911 and 1915, and with Molla Bjurstedt (later Mrs. Mallory) she won it in 1916 and 1917.

Perhaps Eleanora Sears's greatest reputation is as a walker. Once in California she invited a few men to accompany her in a walk up the coast. The men dropped out after a mere 66 miles, while Miss Sears continued without stopping for 108 miles in all. The picture above was taken in the mid-twenties and shows Miss Sears with two friends, Roger W. Cutler (left) and Albert Hinkley (right), on their way from Newport, Rhode Island, to Boston. The men appear to show signs of wear and tear, but not Miss Sears. As recently as 1940 this iron woman made 47 miles in one day, swinging along from Boston to Providence discreetly followed by her chauffeur and limousine. She left Boston at 4 A.M. and arrived in Providence sixteen and a half hours later. Cleveland Amory in his book *The Proper Bostonians* quotes Miss Sears as saying that she doesn't like walking, and does it only for the good of her soul.

At the right you see the redoubtable Eleanora Sears after her defeat in a squash racquets tournament at Merion, Pennsylvania, at the hands of Dot Evans (right), a student at the University of Pennsylvania. The date was March 1946, nearly 40 years from the time the veteran started winning championships.

The first national women's golf tournament was held in the autumn of 1895 on the Meadowbrook course on Long Island. Mrs. Charles S. Brown won with the unimpressive score of 132 for 18 holes. But from then on women's play improved constantly and rapidly, as more and more women played serious golf. An article in the *Outlook* for June 3, 1899, contains the following passage: "Yachtsmen used to wince when they heard the foremast referred to as the 'front post.' . . . But the golfing woman has changed all that, and prides herself on her familiarity with the 'dormies' and 'sclaffs' and 'gobbles' and 'foozles' and all the rest of the jargon in which the golfer is accustomed to expressing himself." What is "sclaff," by the way? Anybody know?

Marion Hollins, who won the national women's golf championship from the famous Alexa Sterling, appears above at what one might describe as the top of her form.

May G. Sutton—later Mrs. Bundy—won the U.S. women's singles tennis championship in 1904 and the English title at Wimbledon the following year. She was the first of the good women players to approach men's style of play. Previous women champions had been content with a defensive, base-line game, relying on steadiness of return and almost never trying for a kill, but May Sutton developed a powerful overhead smash and an aggressive net game. The photograph of her at the left was taken in 1904, the year she won both the women's singles and doubles championship. She had not yet, it appears, followed the advice of Lucille Eaton Hill who wrote in 1903 on tennis dress, "The skirt should be short and stiff enough not to get in the way of the knees or to bend so much around them as to bind or interfere with the player." Other women champions in the pre-World War I era were Hazel V. Hotchkiss (later Mrs. George W. Wightman, donor of the Wightman Cup) and Mary K. Browne. Molla Bjurstedt did not begin her long series of triumphs (eight times women's singles champion) until 1915.

The durability of these early champions commands respectful admiration. Hazel Hotchkiss was four times national singles champion and six times doubles champion in the span between 1909 and 1928; in 1946, Margaret Curtis (who was national champion in 1907) had been playing tournament golf for 53 years; and we have already seen evidence of the lasting power of Miss Eleanora Sears.

the early days of this century, in fact up
til World War I, the average tennis
ayer in the United States was not deeply
cerned with form, or even with any
ticular style of costume for the court.
m was something the champions had,
just plain people didn't go to profes-
nals to learn to play. Nor were they
amed to be seen playing in anything but
ventional white. The young lady at the
t in her bloomers and jacket is display-
the fly-swatter style of play that was
eneral use in 1913 in strictly amateur
les, and who shall say that William
ncan and his leading lady below are
oying themselves any the less because of
solecisms of their attire?

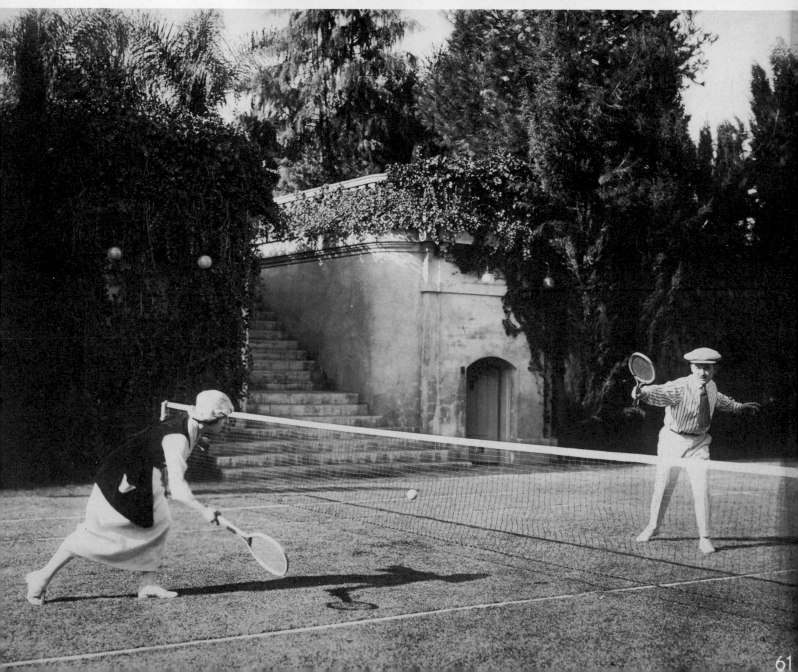

It didn't do the cause of woman suffrage a bit of harm to have anybody as handsome as Inez Milholland working for it, since personal beauty and zeal for reform do not always go together; and Miss Milholland on her white horse got the great Suffrage Parade of October 1915 off to a romantic start on Fifth Avenue, New York.

VOTES FOR WOMEN

The fight for woman suffrage, begun at Seneca Falls, gained momentum in the first decade of the twentieth century despite the fact that the American suffragists were less militant than their opposite numbers in England. By 1900 women could vote in four states, Wyoming, Idaho, Colorado, and Utah, and the election campaign of 1912 showed how solid the gains had been when a number of women delegates attended the Progressive National Convention. By 1916 women had the ballot in eleven states, and in 1919 a bill for woman suffrage was introduced into Congress (fifty-one years after the first such bill) which was ratified the following year as the 19th Amendment—and at last the battle was won.

When Carrie Chapman Catt (above, at the left) became president of the International Suffrage Alliance in 1904, her former post as president of the National American Woman Suffrage Association was filled by Dr. Anna Howard Shaw (standing with Mrs. Catt in the photograph), who remained in office until 1915. Dr. Shaw earned the right to her academic gown and hood by taking degrees in theology and medicine at Boston University. She had had several pastorates when, in 1888, she met Susan B. Anthony and thereafter devoted all her energies and her talents to the cause of woman suffrage.

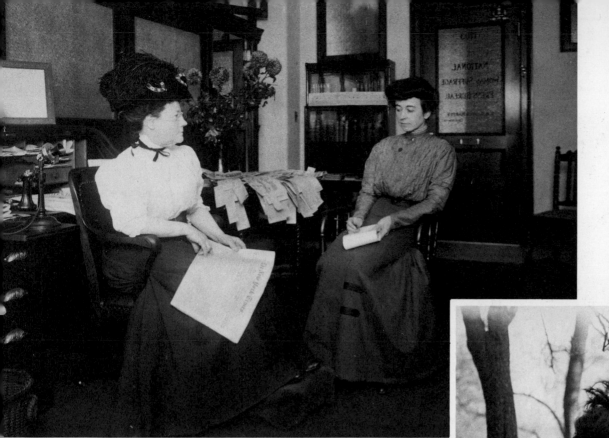

In the photograph above, Ida Husted Harper, the official reporter and historian of the National American Woman Suffrage Association, is at work in the Association's press bureau at 505 Fifth Avenue, New York. The quantity of clippings on the table are evidence both of Miss Harper's diligence and of the fact that suffragettes were sure-fire news. Women won the vote the hard way. They went out and worked for it in the face of discouragement, ridicule, and open hostility. In the lower photograph a resolute worker has penetrated a garage to appeal to the men working there, and at the right, another worker for the cause is selling magazines in the park. The park attendant has apparently accepted the suffrage literature, but as yet remains doubtful.

Opposition to woman suffrage ranged from the satiric drawing above, by Charles Dana Gibson, in which he prophesied a time when there would be women jurors, to the efforts of active anti-suffrage groups. Ex-President Cleveland wrote in an article for the October 1905 issue of the *Ladies' Home Journal*, "Sensible and responsible women do not want to vote. The relative positions to be assumed by man and woman in the working out of our civilization were assigned long ago by a higher intelligence than ours." Meanwhile the suffragettes continued working doggedly and with a confidence that is reflected in the picture below, which shows a group of women in Chicago, preparing themselves for the privileges of full citizenship by practising casting votes by means of a voting machine.

POLLING PLACE

WOMEN IN OFFICE

The suffrage victory failed to infuse American politics with a new righteousness, as many ardent suffrage orators, in their conviction that women were morally superior to men, had predicted it would. Nor, for that matter, has there ever been such a thing as "the woman's vote." But it was an essential step toward complete recognition that women were people, with all the rights and responsibilities thereof. It failed to fill the country with swarms of professional women politicians, as others had foretold; a quarter of a century and more later, there was still only a small sprinkling of women among the members of Congress—and there has been to date (1948) only one woman Cabinet member. And this despite the fact that some of these politicos were (and are) highly competent—and, moreover, far more personable than the hypothetical female politician depicted by the cartoonists of the Gibson era. Above, left, is Representative Edith Nourse Rogers of Massachusetts; below, Representative Clare Boothe Luce as she looked in 1944, in conversation with John Gunther and (right) the indomitable Elsa Maxwell, who, in her time, has organized quite a few parties herself, only they weren't political; above, right, is Representative Helen Gahagan Douglas of California. (When, in 1944, the Republicans featured ex-playwright Mrs. Luce as a convention spellbinder, the Democrats countered with ex-actress Mrs. Douglas.)

Many of the suffragists went on to public office. Above, left, is Mrs. J. Borden Harriman, leading the Washington ambulance corps in a Red Cross parade in 1917; just below you will see her on shipboard when—some twenty years later—she was Minister to Norway. Another diplomat, Ruth Bryan Owen (whose father was William Jennings Bryan), is shown above being sworn in as Minister to Denmark and Iceland in 1933. Below is the first woman member of the Cabinet, Frances Perkins, conversing as Secretary of Labor with the top rank labor leaders, William Green of the A.F. of L. (left) and Philip Murray of the C.I.O.

Others wielded great influence in public affairs without holding public office, as did the two cousins on this page. The long-legged child with the horse wrote, years later, "I was tall, very thin, and very shy." She married the young man with the pince-nez shown driving with her below (along with Mr. and Mrs. Herbert L. Satterlee). Both cousins achieved distinguished reputations in their own right, regardless of their residence in the White House. You've guessed it—the name is Roosevelt.

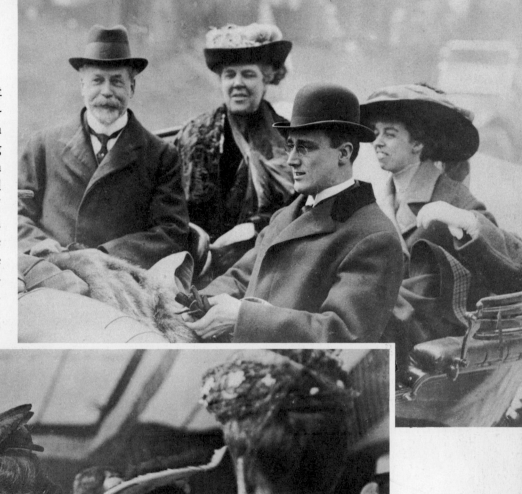

The pretty girl below in the feathered hat who is chatting so animatedly is at a wedding reception in the Philippines. Her own wedding to Nicholas Longworth, a young congressman from Ohio, took place on February 17, 1906, and it was remarked that a shade of blue named "Alice blue" in honor of the bride was conspicuous in the costumes of the women guests. In the same year a popular song, "Alice, Where Art Thou Going?" referred to her excessive fondness for travel. A family characteristic, perhaps?

We have remarked that the suffrage movement in this country was marked by far less public disturbance than in England. There were firebrands, however, among the ranks of labor. Mother Jones (above, right) closed her profitable dressmaking business in 1877 during a railroad strike to join forces with the workers. Throughout her ninety-odd years she remained an incendiary and a strong believer in literal class warfare. She wrote in 1925, "Many of our modern leaders of labor have wandered far from the thorny paths of these early crusaders. Never in the early days of the labor struggle would you find leaders wining and dining with the aristocracy; nor did their wives strut about like diamond-bedecked peacocks; nor were they attended by humiliated, cringing, colored servants. . . ." Elizabeth Gurley Flynn (right) followed in her footsteps. The daughter of an early "wobbly," she employed her Irish eloquence as a leader in the I.W.W. and was active in the violent textile strike in Lawrence, Massachusetts, in 1912.

A different type was Rose Schneiderman, shown above at a Women's Trade Union League Meeting in New York. A highly effective speaker, she did not depend on oratory for results, but—like Agnes Nestor and Fannia M. Cohn—studied economics and law, and became not only a spokesman for labor but a representative of labor as a social group.

Emma Goldman (*left*), vehement Communist and advocate of free love, was a stormy petrel until she was deported to her native Russia in 1920 for obstructing military conscription. In this photograph she appears to be completely unmoved by the beauty of the lilies.

PHILANTHROPY VS. REFORM

The period that showed the blossoming of woman as companion-and-rival-to-man—the first decades of the twentieth century—was also a time when the social worker came into her own. It was a time of reform and various agencies were established with opportunities for women workers. Many college graduates who had rebelled at the idea of teaching, and who were animated with a zeal for social betterment for their fellow-men, eagerly entered this new profession.

The tradition of the sheltered lady included good works and charitable gestures, and many women of wealth were known to be seriously concerned with the lot of the less fortunate. A few gave generously and wisely. Mrs. Finley Shepard (left, above) was unsparing of effort and money, and Mrs. Russell Sage was reported to have given some $80 millions to welfare, hospitals, and the Russell Sage Foundation. She is shown above, contributing to the welfare of a squirrel. But the social worker who worked for improving the conditions of the poor rather than alleviating the results of the conditions followed a new school. Miss Jane Addams, at the right, was a memorable figure in this movement. From the time she founded Hull House in 1889, the settlement had a great influence in the civic life of Chicago, particularly in connection with the assimilation of the city's foreign-born citizens.

Americans have always been a restless lot. "Are you going somewhere, or just traveling?" was a common greeting in the West. The Europe-bound travelers of 1899 in A. B. Wenzell's drawing above would have applauded the decision of the passengers on the Grace Line's "Santa Rosa" in the nineteen-forties to take a Caribbean cruise, although they might have wondered at their clothes. The family at the right is touring Wyoming in 1925.

But many Americans have always preferred, when summer arrived, to go to one place and stay there. Before many families even among the well-to-do had "summer places" and while Newport was still a quiet seaport town frequented during the warm months by unostentatious intellectuals, those who could afford a lavish holiday swarmed to the spas, where after the European fashion they could drink mineral waters or take sulphur baths while in residence at large and fashionable hotels. In the drawing above from *Frank Leslie's Illustrated Newspaper* for July 19, 1879, you see "a Fifth Avenue belle superintending the packing of her Saratoga trunk." Clearly she is bound for the greatest of the northern spas, Saratoga Springs. The two pictures below were taken—some years apart—at a resort described by Baedeker in 1899 as follows: "For nearly a century the Greenbrier White Sulphur Springs have been the typical resort of the wealth and aristocracy of the South; and the pictures of Southern life, beauty, and fashion still seen here will be found of great interest by the European or Northern visitor." It will be noted that the ladies of the present day, although attired more revealingly, do not seem at the moment to be attracting any such masculine attention as is manifested by the gallant at the left in the older picture.

Baedeker in 1899 named Newport the "Undisputed Queen of American Seaside Resorts," and it seems unlikely that anyone would cavil at this term. The palaces (termed "cottages") of marble or limestone, copied after Renaissance chateaux or Italian villas, seem oddly unsuited to the rocky New England coast, but there is no denying that Newport represented for a great many years the very citadel of American social and financial power. It was at Newport that William R. Travers, noted wit and financier, made one of his most famous remarks. Henry Clews in his book, *Fifty Years in Wall Street*, tells how Travers took a party of friends to watch a yacht race: "Casting his eyes across the glittering water, he beheld a number of beautiful white-winged yachts in the distance, and finding, by inquiry, that they all belonged to well known Wall Street brokers, he appeared thereby to be thrown momentarily into a deep reverie, and, without turning his gaze from the handsome squadron, finally asked, 'Wh-wh-where are the cu-cu-customers' yachts?' "

The photograph below, taken in the early nineteen-hundreds, shows an automobile show in progress. A look at the top hats and elaborate dresses carries the conviction that in those days Newport stood for style—high, wide, and handsome—and reminds us how far we have come from strict formality in dress.

Some people have always yearned for the attractions of nature—as in the pictures on this page. We cannot, unfortunately, pin them down precisely as to time or place; but at any rate they demonstrate the perpetual hunger of certain holiday-makers for living in tents, getting their feet wet in the ocean, or standing on rocks in lakes.

The heyday of the summer hotel has long since passed. Nowadays a prosperous or moderately prosperous family in one of our cities is likely to have a summer place—house, cottage, camp, shack, farm, or ranch—of its own to which the mother and the children repair for three months or so, while the father comes for a briefer vacation, and also, if the distance is not too great, for strenuous week-ends. At the beginning of the century comparatively few families had two establishments; a standard practice was for the family to select a summer hotel and move to it *en masse* (taking with them a number of trunks) for a fortnight or a month or six weeks. Above you will see the guests at a hotel at Blue Mountain Lake in the Adirondacks crowding to the edge of the wide porch to witness the departure of other guests by stagecoach to the train. Below is a somewhat later view of another hotel porch (probably called a *piazza*)—the place where one strolled out to look at the weather or sat in rocking chairs to gossip and comment on the passersby, or dozed while recovering from a monumental American-Plan dinner.

Harper's Weekly for July 23, 1892, says of Gray Gables, "The builder was generous with piazzas, and if it is too cold on the seaward side, it is warmer on the other. . . . There is no pretence of decoration. Everything is shining pine, the walls and ceilings as well as the floors. There is no paint, no color but that of the yellow wood and the rough stone of the chimneys." In architectural style, this type of ample seaside cottage is pure American, and whatever its aesthetic value, it provided the most comfortable kind of living.

The pictures on this page show three examples of the American summer place: the chalet-like structure above stood just outside Clinton, New York; the drawing at the right is of Grover Cleveland's Cape Cod house, Gray Gables; and, just to bring us up to the present, Constance Bennett's Malibu beach house appears below,

Baedeker's *United States* (1899) contains this comment on the customs of the country: "Sea-bathing in the United States differs somewhat from British and Continental practices. Permanent bathhouses on the beach take the place of bathing coaches, and the institution of bathing masters is almost unknown. Men and women bathe together. The temperature of the water of the Atlantic in summer is so warm that bathers frequently remain in it an hour or more, apparently without harm."

Some people stayed at home. The upper photograph is a perfect expression of the quiet summer life in a small town in 1900. The lower one, taken in the same year, pictures a family reunion.

City dwellers in the United States, in the nineties, while perhaps not so well equipped with public places for outdoor recreation as their counterparts in Europe, nevertheless made the most of what they had. The children at the left are playing ball in New York's Central Park. The center photograph shows Coney Island in 1896. Various Atlantic seashore resorts, once fashionable, lost their prestige as Society moved to other places. Asbury Park and Atlantic City are notable examples. But from the beginning Coney Island never had any claim to style.

These two photographs of Coney Island, taken some fifty years apart, remind us of some of the factors that have changed New York life in that period—growth of population, improved means of rapid transit, and notable changes in the convention of dress.

The spacious West has for long been an Eden for the hardy souls who take pleasure in camping and big game hunting, as well as for the gentler souls who like nature in the large. (It was estimated that two and a half million visitors enjoyed the beauty of our national parks in the year 1928, and the number has risen considerably since then.) It is interesting to observe, however, that in recent years the rigors of Western vacations have lessened to a marked degree. At Sun Valley, Idaho, for example, every luxury and comfort may be found. The young lady at the left is being effortlessly conveyed up the mountain in a chair-type ski lift. Not content with the usual seasonal sports, this resort offers swimming in warmed water pools in winter, and skating on artificial ice in summer. Visitors to the Flying L Ranch in Texas (lower picture) don't have to bother with common carriers; the ranch has a flying field for those who come by private plane.

Palm Springs, California (right), dear to the hearts of Hollywood stars, is California's most glittering winter resort. Other people can go, too, if their bank accounts can stand it. And Florida offers an endless variety of spots for fugitives from winter. Ponte Vedra (below) is a comparatively new resort. Prices of deluxe travel today are undeniably high; $40 to $50 a day for basic accommodations for two is not unusual. Time was when, according to a writer in *McCall's* for August 1913, a delightful vacation could be made by trolley for very much less. "For the more adventurous spirit," she says, "with $25 or $30 in her pocket, it is entirely possible to trolley from Chicago to New York." The trip took from three to four days, but one was advised to allow a week each way for stop-overs, since "The real joy of a trolley trip lies in the leisurely travel it permits."

WOMEN AND WAR

The picture at right is called "Rumors of War," and since it was painted by W. T. Smedley in 1898, the title clearly refers to the Spanish-American War. The scene shows the interior of a typical comfortable American house of the time. The husband's expression is grave but not alarmed. The wife may rely on him for sound judgment and a clear explanation of the significance of the news. The little boy in his Lord Fauntleroy suit is peacefully and busily playing with toy soldiers.

At the left is a group of nurses on board the hospital ship "Relief" at Siboney, Cuba; and below is another group of nurses with convalescent soldiers at Camp Thomas, Chickamauga Park, Georgia. Both photographs are dated 1898. Women's participation in the Spanish-American War was confined to nursing.

The picture changed in World War I. Not only did the Red Cross provide countless stations where women came to knit helmets, wristlets, socks, and sweaters, and to roll bandages, but women, to some degree, took the places of men in offices and factories, and the Navy, stronghold of conservatism, opened the door to some 11,000 who enlisted as Yeomen (F), USNR, the (F) standing for female. A few of them appear below. To be sure, the nurses were still by far the most important feminine contingent, and the photograph at the left, above, shows Col. Julia C. Stimson receiving the Distinguished Service Medal from the hands of General Pershing at Tours, France. Miss Stimson, chief of the American Red Cross nursing service in France, was in charge of some 11,000 nurses, and was the first woman to hold an officer's rank in the Army Nurse Corps. She was made a major in 1920, and later elevated to the rank of colonel. At her right, you see Ruth Law, pioneer aviator, in the uniform in which she flew over the Western Front. Mary Pickford (at the extreme right, above) was the doughboys' favorite movie actress. In this picture, she is welcoming returning soldiers of the 143rd Field Artillery, of Oakland, California.

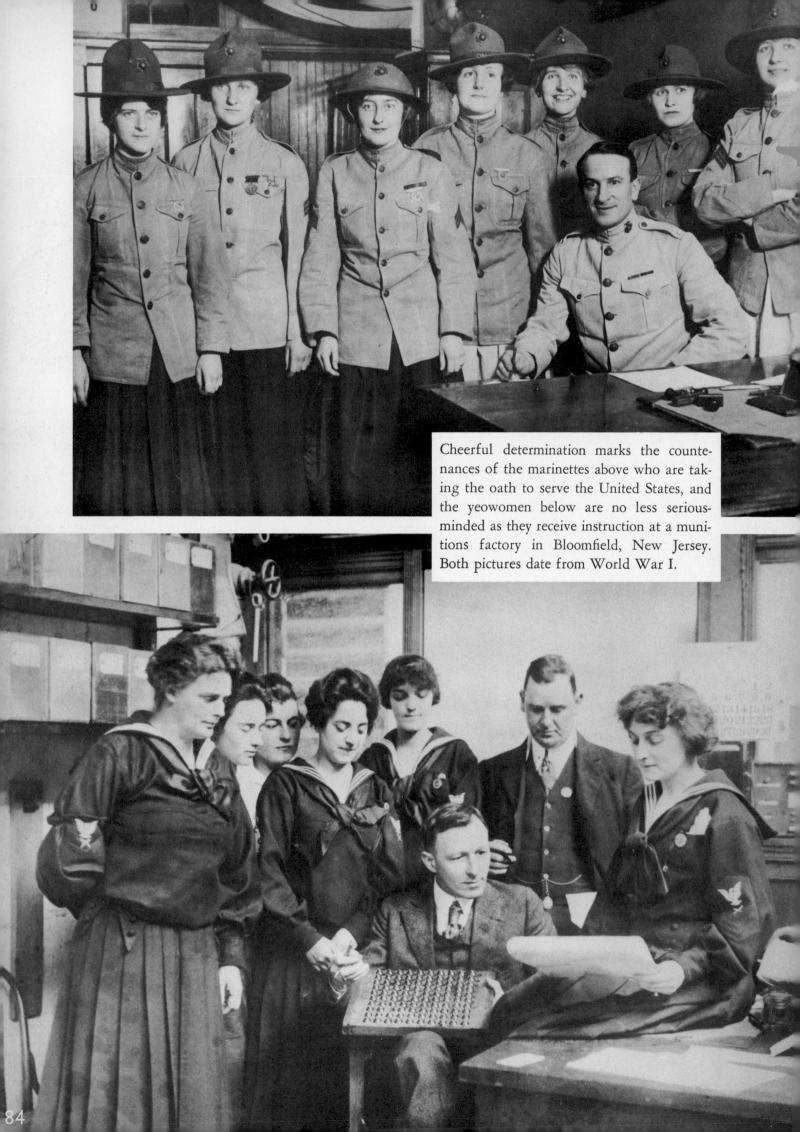

Cheerful determination marks the countenances of the marinettes above who are taking the oath to serve the United States, and the yeowomen below are no less serious-minded as they receive instruction at a munitions factory in Bloomfield, New Jersey. Both pictures date from World War I.

It's very easy to laugh at the photographs of women in World War I, but one must remember several things as one compares the pictures on the foregoing pages with those on this page. For one thing, photography made great strides in twenty-three years. Also the women's uniforms in World War II were designed with great care and skill. Another item is that in 1941-45 the people of the United States made an effort which, while it may not have been all-out, was much more nearly total than ever before, and whereas in World War I a number of earnest but not noticeably attractive girls got into uniforms, a generation later it was distinctly "the thing" to have an active part in the war effort. The four girls at the right represent four women's branches of the armed services. From left to right they are wearing the uniform of the U. S. Army Nurse Corps, the U. S. Navy Nurse Corps, the WAVES (Women Assigned to Voluntary Emergency Service), and the WAACS (Women's Army Auxiliary Corps). Below you see Capt. Newton White, USN (Ret.), and Lt. Commander Mildred McAfee, Director of the Women's Reserve of the Navy, reviewing a group of enlisted WAVES at the U. S. Naval Air Station in Brooklyn, New York.

Between two and three per cent of the United States armed forces in World War II were women, the total number being close to 400,000. They were assigned to innumerable domestic posts and to all the major theatres of operations in the world. They did not engage in combat or perform tasks for which they were physically unfit, but so diverse is modern warfare that there were thousands of necessary tasks and operations which women could, and did, perform quite as well as men. A random selection of Army and Navy posts held by women includes X-ray technician, public relations expert, motion picture projectionist, photographer, draftsman, radio operator, weather observer, mechanic, sheet metal worker, welder, armament inspector, aviation mechanic's mate, truck driver, printer, and control tower operator. The WAAC above, running the tractor, is guiding a transient aircraft into place on the flight line, and the Marine below is a second lieutenant in charge of records, having previously studied drafting at Carnegie Tech in Pittsburgh.

The WAVES at the right, working on the engine of a scout trainer, are aviation metalsmiths. They are only two of many thousands of American women who were taught hitherto undreamed-of skills by the global war. The members of the Women's Reserve of the Coast Guard took their name—SPARS—from the Coast Guard's motto and its translation, "Semper Paratus, Always Ready." Lower shows three SPAR officers on board a Coast Guard cutter in Alaska. First director of the SPARS was Captain Dorothy C. Stratton, corresponding to Colonel Oveta Culp Hobby of the WAACS, Lt. Commander Mildred McAfee Horton of the WAVES, and Colonel Ruth Cheney Streeter of the Marines.

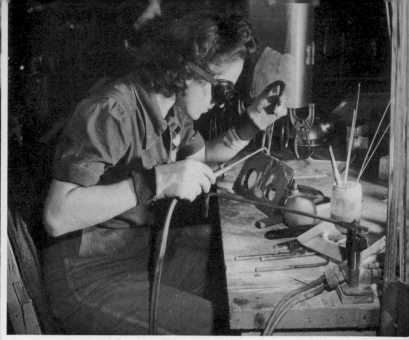

Not only the armed services but also the Red Cross, munitions plants, and government offices offered women chances to take an active part in the war effort. The Red Cross girls at the left are handing out doughnuts, candy, cigarettes, and general cheer to British soldiers arriving in Naples from the Anzio beachhead. The welder above was one of the 169,000 women in aircraft plants. And there were dozens of offices in Washington like the one below in the Priorities Division of the War Production Board.

These girls are inspecting parachutes that have come back from a test flight.

We have seen women in the armed forces, in the Red Cross, in war plants, in the offices of the vast emergency agencies. There was another area in which they contributed to the war effort—by taking civilian jobs that released men for fighting. Working on the railroad and driving taxicabs are not usual feminine occupations, but the women on this page appear to be making out just fine.

It is interesting to look over the advertising pages in the periodicals of the war years and see how general was the assumption that American women were engaged in some kind of war work. Occasionally the effort to tie in the product with the essential task produced a bizarre result, as in the copy for a lipstick advertisement that read, "It's a reflection of the free democratic way of life that you have succeeded in keeping your femininity—even though you are doing a man's work! . . . No lipstick—ours or anyone else's—will win the war. But it symbolizes one of the reasons why we are fighting . . . the precious right of women to be feminine and lovely—under any circumstances." Sweet are the uses of democracy!

So far we have been considering women and war in terms of full-time, paid occupations. There isn't room in this kind of book to list the variety or quantity of activities that women engaged in on a volunteer, part-time basis. They ranged from working in hospitals as nurses' aids to entertaining foreign seamen, from taking First Aid courses to driving generals. Two farm women in Maryland at the right are serving as airplane spotters; the group below are at work in the Lithuanian Chapter of the Red Cross in Pittsburgh. The job of air raid warden (organized in anticipation of enemy bombings) occupied many women who cheerfully undertook night duty at sector or zone headquarters although their days were filled with office or domestic work. Air raid wardens worried about ways of handling high explosive, incendiary, fragmentation, and gas bombs; when to use sand, and when to resort to the stirrup pump; what to do when Signal 50 should come; which gas it was that smelled like marigolds; what to do with people who left lights on in a test blackout. They also struggled with hypothetical incidents and prepared themselves bravely to cope with a concocted situation such as this: "A water main has been broken by H.E. bomb. The street is flooded. An elderly crippled man lives in the basement of No. 245. Fire has broken out in No. 247, and there is looting in the store at No. 246. What to do first?"

FASHION REVIEW

1894

1903

Looking at the fashion drawings on these two pages, one is forced to admit that there is nothing static about the feminine form. To be sure these are drawings, but granted that the pen is mightier than the flesh, there is ample photographic evidence to prove my point.

1913

1920

1926

1934

The celebrated New Look of the autumn of 1947 was
nowhere as radical a change in styles as the one that
came about in the early thirties when the waist came
out of hiding, the bosom returned, shoulders squared
themselves, and the neckline rose as the hem descended.

1940

1948

THE EXPANDING—AND EXPANSIVE—TWENTIES

A great change in the status and attitudes of American women was impending at the time of World War I (1917-18). It was a complex change, gradual and very uneven. One must never forget that there is a great variety of social codes and assumptions and behavior among different communities of the United States, among different groups in each community, and among different individuals in each group. At any moment in the nineteen-twenties, for example, one could find in almost every American town women who were by training and inclination sheltered ladies, others who were companions and rivals of man, and others who represented the newer trends. And if the ratification of the Suffrage Amendment in 1919 climaxed the period when the companion and rival of man had been most clearly in the ascendancy, already for years before 1919 the new ferments had been at work. Yet the change which was brewing was widespread and pervasive. It was to produce during the nineteen-twenties three characteristic new types—the sophisticate, the flapper, and the careerist—representing three striking impulses: the desire to be worldly, the quest of pleasure at the expense of Mrs. Grundy, and the ambition to win a personal success in business or other occupations. To generalize in the broadest way, one might say that the American woman, having broken away from the shelter that had protected her mother, and being assured of the status that had been won for her by her older sister, proceeded to cash in on her new advantages—to enjoy her social and intellectual freedom, to have a good time even if she shocked the neighbors, and to get on in the world for her own satisfaction.

The changes transformed her very appearance, and the transformation was especially sharp in the years between 1920 and 1926, as you will see from the fashion drawings on the next few pages. To feel its full impact, do not simply compare the clothes of one time with those of the next, but consider what sort of impression the fashion artists of different periods thought their customers wanted to convey. The drawing at the right, from the April 1, 1926, issue of *Vogue*, shows an evening cape from the Patou collection, made of white Georgette crêpe with deep silk fringe; it also shows the type of *soignée* woman of the world that was admired at the time.

John Held, Jr., immortalized the flapper. His drawing below appeared in the April 15, 1926, issue of *Life*. Dorothy Shaver, whose photograph (a recent one) is at the upper right, is a notable example of what the ambitious girl of the twenties might hope to achieve. Her career at Lord & Taylor, New York department store, began in 1924, when she joined the store as head of the comparison department, and so brilliant was her performance that in three years she was made a director.

Dorothy Shaver, president of Lord & Taylor, is the first woman in the history of retail merchandising to head a $40 million corporation. She has contributed many new ideas in store management and has been largely responsible for the growth of the fashion industry in the United States.

There was a time when the gap between the clothes of a woman of fashion and those of an everyday woman was so great that even the untutored eye could tell the difference at a glance. High style was for the very few, and most American women—even those with money—were nervous about what they called "extreme" clothes. Paris set the styles, to be sure, but they were sharply modified for most Americans. The *McCall* patterns—and other patterns—were designed to meet the moderate skills of women who made their own clothes or superintended the local dressmaker, and who would not have thought of themselves as belonging to the world of fashion. The two groups of evening clothes on this page both date from 1919, but there's a vast difference between them, both in actual style and in presentation. The French models at the right appeared in the May 1 issue of *Vogue*. Below is a page from B. Altman's catalogue of 1919. The big department store carried French models for its metropolitan customers, but they did not appear in the catalogue which was mailed to out-of-towners.

The dithyrambs of fashion reporting are sometimes wonderful indeed. The caption for the group above reads, "When a slender satin frock (left) depends entirely upon the curving lines of neck and skirt—a skirt slit on either side to the silken knee—then indeed those lines must be French, and here they are of Lanvin's designing. A double apron gives its cold jet glitter for the gown's only adornment. The middle gown, . . . with greater extravagance, has completely covered the satin underslip with a net overdress heavily embroidered with jet. . . . There is something less of dignified composure in the next frock of satin and net. A certain coquetry lurks in the flounces of jet, a certain pert insouciance flashes from the jet fringes . . . and heavy strands of jet beads accent the whiteness of those restless French shoulders."

IMPORTED UNDERGARMENTS

48S26 Nightrobe of Laundered Batiste. Philippine hand-embroidery; hand-sewn. Sizes 14, 15 and 16 inches $3.90
48S27 Corset Cover of Laundered Nainsook, French hand-embroidery (assorted patterns). Sizes 36, 38, 40 and 42 inches, bust measurement $2.25
48S28 Drawers of Laundered Nainsook, French hand-embroidery (assorted patterns). Lengths 21 and 23 inches $2.25
48S29 Nightrobe of Laundered Batiste, hand-sewn; Philippine hand-embroidery. Sizes 14, 15 and 16 inches $2.65

48S30 Nightrobe of Laundered Batiste, hand-sewn; Philippine embroidery. Sizes 14, 15 and 16 inches . . . . $
48S31 Petticoat of Nainsook, French hand-embroidery (assorted patterns). Lengths 36 and 38 inches . . . . $
48S32 Drawer Combination of Laundered Nainsook, French hand-embroidery (assorted patterns). Sizes 36, 38 and 40 inches, bust measurement . . . $

As the garments shown on this page are imported, and the supply limited, it may be necessary in some instances to substitute patterns slightly different.

There is little that is striking to our eyes about the two dresses above (from *McCall's* for February 1920) except that the one on the right seems unduly fussy, and neither seems to fit very well. But the two groups displaying lingerie strike one today as distinctly odd. The ladies are modestly shapeless, for one thing, not because the flat, straight-up-and-down figure was yet fashionable, but because the convention of the time was less bold than that of the present. The group at the upper right are wearing handmade garments of batiste or nainsook with Philippine embroidery, those at the right are wearing crêpe de chine or georgette, largely machine-made—a less conservative choice in 1919, when these drawings were made. (Both pictures of lingerie illustrate merchandise from B. Altman.) The prices of the fine cotton underwear, for all their hand work, ran rather below those for the silk; the nightgowns in the upper group ran from $3.10 to $3.90, the drawers and corset cover were $2.25 each, whereas the fancy combination worn by the lady in the boudoir cap below cost $16.75, and the pyjamas on the seated figure were priced at $6.90.

Not a grand dress, but a "little" chiffon frock, illustrated in the April 15, 1926, issue of *Vogue*, featuring "chic simplicity and skilful cut." It was made of indigo blue chiffon, with a cluster of pink roses at the left hip. Notice the numerous bracelets, the big earrings, and the pearl choker. This was a Renée model, imported by B. Altman, New York department store.

By 1926, the gap between high style and everyday style which we mentioned on page 95 had diminished noticeably. French frocks still had exquisite handmade detail and a mastery of cut that Miss Carrie or Miss Susie who came by the day could hardly hope to equal, but Mrs. Smith of Main Street wanted to create the same impression as Mrs. Smith of Park Avenue and the Faubourg St. Honoré, and the deceptive simplicity of the little chemise frocks that were the uniform of the smart woman was much easier to make a stab at than the intricate draperies of an earlier day. The drawing at the left from the April 1, 1926, issue of *Vogue* shows a Louiseboulanger model imported by Wanamaker. The three drawings below are *McCall* patterns, published in the January 1926 issue of that magazine. In the captions of both, there is emphasis on the new "flying movement" in clothes. There is even a new word for it—"kinetic."

The diagonal line of figures below appeared in Altman's catalogue for September 1926, and
the bottom drawing shows what
had happened to women's figures by 1940—and also to the
artists' code of etiquette.

No wonder the women of the nineties had small waists and sat up
straight. The corset at the upper right may not have been America's
favorite by scientific poll count, but it, or something like it, was
worn by most women. Unyielding fabric and strong whalebone kept
the wearer rigid, and the lacings at the back, adjusted by a strong-
armed maid or sister after the corset was hooked in front, fixed the
circumference of the waist at the very minimum the victim could
endure. An 18-inch waist was a mark of great bodily beauty. Undoubtedly memories of such tortures had something to do with the
radical change in figures that came in about 1919 when the uncor-
seted look was desirable, and the small waist despised. At that time
the perfect figure showed a difference of only four inches between
waist and hips. (Nine to eleven inches difference is characteristic
of the current model's figure.)

These two pages show Hollywood stars in the fashions of the twenties. Do you recognize Loretta Young above or Barbara Worth below?

Bessie Love (*above*) in beige silk has the oddly foreshortened silhouette that was fashionable in 1929, and Bebe Daniels prepares for tennis.

Marian Nixon wore this crystal and silver beaded evening dress in 1927. The dress worn by Jean Arthur in 1929 foreshadows the longer skirt.

Ruth Taylor (*above*) wore a brief dancing frock of filmy chiffon. Two years later Kay Francis' eggshell velvet had panels and a train.

The movies offer an admirable opportunity to study our contention as to the lag in the acceptance of emerging types. Mary Pickford, the darling of the cinema audiences throughout the twenties, was no flapper, sophisticate, or career girl. "America's Sweetheart" was the little girl with long curls who was sweetly brave through adversity, as in *Pollyanna* (*below*) in which she made a great hit in 1920. You can see how really lovely she was from the close-up above. Mary Pickford had begun her movie career in a picture called *The New York Hat*. Griffith had bought the story for fifteen dollars from a San Diego high-school girl named Anita Loos, and the male lead was played by a young actor named Lionel Barrymore.

Mary Pickford's immense popularity did not mean that the movies appealed only to one's better self. Sin flourished too (before the Parent Teachers Association got busy) and in 1917 Theda Bara, having immortalized the vamp in *A Fool There Was*, appeared as Cleopatra in the striking get-up shown at the right. Would it be carping to suggest that she rather overdid the serpent motif? There was plenty of passion too, when Rudolph Valentino was on the screen. He appears below, left, with Nazimova in a scene from *Camille*, in which both players are registering intense feeling, and at the right, in the memorable picture of 1921 —*The Four Horsemen of the Apocalypse*. At the bottom, Gloria Swanson, a former Mack Sennett bathing beauty, appears in a scene from *Male and Female* (produced in 1919). She has already made a good start on those fabulous costumes that became her trademark.

Pearl White, queen of the serials, went through some pretty shattering times in *The Perils of Pauline* in 1920 and even in *Plunder*, made in 1923, things weren't any too easy for her—as the picture below clearly illustrates. Mae Murray, on the other hand, is just as clearly having a splendid time waltzing with John Gilbert in *The Merry Widow*, which Eric von Stroheim directed in 1925. John Gilbert was by this time on his way to becoming one of the screen's great lovers, a position he achieved when he was teamed with Greta Garbo in such pictures as *The Flesh and the Devil, Love, A Woman of Affairs,* and *Queen Christina.*

To many people in the twenties, Clara Bow was the perfect embodiment of the flapper. She is shown at the right in *Children of Divorce* in 1927, the same year she was made the "it" girl by Elinor Glyn. The tall young man standing beside her is Gary Cooper.

Joan Crawford got her first big chance in a picture called *Our Dancing Daughters*, a product of the flaming-youth school of movies. This was in 1928, still before talking pictures had arrived. Her first all-talking picture was *Untamed*, made in 1929, in which a young actor named Robert Montgomery, newly come to Hollywood, played opposite her. Who would have thought that the madcap dancer above, whose Charleston was unsurpassed, would turn into the handsome distinguished woman at the right? She did, though; this is Joan Crawford in *Possessed*.

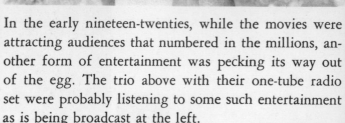

In the early nineteen-twenties, while the movies were attracting audiences that numbered in the millions, another form of entertainment was pecking its way out of the egg. The trio above with their one-tube radio set were probably listening to some such entertainment as is being broadcast at the left.

The picture above shows Dr. Vladimir Zworykin demonstrating his new cathode ray television set in the late nineteen-twenties. A modern television set is shown at the left.

OCCUPATIONS—TRADITIONAL AND NEW

We have already mentioned the careerist as an emerging type in the heady twenties. Numerically she was not impressive, but the feeling was in the air and ambitious girls flocked to the cities—notably to New York—to set the world afire. Some of them followed well worn trails, and the stage was still the most glamorous of all careers. The Theatre Guild, organized in 1919 by a little theatre group called the Washington Square Players, introduced a fresh note of experiment into Broadway, and launched Eugene O'Neill, Katharine Cornell, and other ranking theatrical names. One of the sprightliest of comediennes of the twenties was Ina Claire, seen at the right in *The Last of Mrs. Cheyney*, in 1925. She had formerly been one of the leads in the *Ziegfeld Follies*, and just to show how people change, we've included a picture of her at the right below as she appeared in *The Quaker Girl* while she was still a musical comedy star in 1912.

In 1919 William Gillette starred in a play called *Dear Brutus*. He was highly praised as usual but a young girl in the part of Margaret romped off with the honors. You see them below, and you undoubtedly recognize Helen Hayes.

The high standards of accomplishment set by American women writers of an earlier period were easily maintained during the literary flowering of the twenties. The eight women whose pictures appear on this page and the next represent a goodly company and serve to illustrate the variety and range of women's abilities in a single field. Willa Cather's remarkable novels, *O Pioneers* and *My Antonia*, were published before the twenties, but she gained her great reputation in that decade with the Pulitzer-prize-winning *One of Ours* (1922) and *A Lost Lady* (1923). Miss Cather is shown at the left, above, and below her is Ellen Glasgow, whose first popular success, *The Voice of the People*, appeared in 1900, and who reached the top of her form in 1926 in *The Romantic Comedians*. Miss Glasgow was the first Southern writer to rebel against the magnolia-and-mocking-bird treatment of the South which had been accepted practice among authors. Mary Roberts Rinehart (below) has so many successful books to her name that Irving Harlow Hart puts her on the top of his list of authors of best sellers for the past fifty years. The *Red Lamp* was a notable hit in 1925. Pearl Buck (above) made literary history with *The Good Earth*, which won the Pulitzer Prize in 1931.

Edna St. Vincent Millay (*top*) and Amy Lowell (*above, right*) rank as two of America's most distinguished poets. Miss Lowell was a continuous experimenter with verse forms, but her fine biography of John Keats, published in 1925, was written with classic purity. Miss Millay, who was a full-fledged poet even before she went to Vassar, provided the younger generation of the twenties with a motto they tried hard to live by when she wrote, "My candle burns at both ends. . . ." Dorothy Parker (*above*) also caught the spirit of the twenties. She was unsurpassed at ironic light verse, with a particular gift for the surprise ending and the inspired title. *Enough Rope* appeared in 1926. Edna Ferber (in the recent photograph at the right), a master story-teller, established herself firmly in the top ranks with *So Big* in 1924 and has stayed there ever since.

The concept that the American women are guardians of the arts while men work hard, make money, and generally run things is a time-honored one. There's another implication as well: men paint the pictures and collect them; women look at them and appreciate them. In the group below who are earnestly studying French painting, there is one man visible. The woman who is explaining the pictures illustrates an occupation that is comparatively new—conducting classes in art appreciation in our metropolitan museums. The lady at the right, Isabella Stewart Gardner, broke all the rules about men being the great art collectors. Mrs. John L. Gardner was one of Boston's great ladies, as highly civilized as she was wildly unpredictable. She built a Venetian palace, with a great inner courtyard in which fountains played and flowering trees scented the air, and she filled it with magnificent paintings by the old masters to form a museum of unique beauty, which she bequeathed to the city of Boston. She was a pioneer and leading influence in a generation of such great collectors as Morgan, Frick, Huntington, and Mellon. Gertrude Vanderbilt Whitney was another important influence in her own fashion. A sculptor herself, Mrs. Whitney was aware of the difficulties that beset the young and unknown artist. She founded the Whitney Studio Gallery and the Whitney Studio Club to assist artists of talent—giving them a place to show their work and an opportunity to meet with other artists. The Whitney Museum of American Art grew out of these institutions, and was opened to the public in 1931.

Early in 1942, when the American Women's Association gave a testimonial dinner to Anne Morgan, the guest of honor posed for the picture above with two other women distinguished in other fields. Miss Morgan (*center*), daughter of the great banker J. Pierpont Morgan, had made her high reputation as a philanthropist, but not of the remote Lady Bountiful variety. She had not been content with writing checks for good causes organized by others. She had been an organizer and an energizer. Her interest in working conditions had led her to join the Women's Trade Union League; she had once served as a sanitary inspector in a factory; as head of the American Committee for Devastated France, she had run a huge enterprise of mercy during World War I and the years that followed; and in 1939 she had organized the American Friends of France to help women and children who were victims of the ravages of World War II. With Miss Morgan in this picture are (left) Anne O'Hare McCormick, leading newspaperwoman, whose dispatches to the *New York Times* have won for her international respect; and (right) Rachel Crothers, accomplished playwright, noted for her social comedies.

We have already spoken of teaching as a traditional form of woman's work, but not a great number of women get to be college presidents. Among those who have proved themselves able to administer large educational enterprises is Sarah Blanding, who in the nineteen-twenties, at the University of Kentucky, was shifting her principal interest from physical education (she had won a certificate of the New Haven Normal School of Gymnastics in 1919) to political science, and was serving as the University's dean of women. The picture above was taken after her election as the first woman president of Vassar College in 1946.

Still rare are women scientists of top rank, or important women business executives, or top-flight lawyers. But Dr. Florence Sabin (*above, left*), who in the early nineteen-twenties was professor of histology at Johns Hopkins, and from 1925 to 1938 worked at the Rockefeller Institute for Medical Research, discovered the origin of the type of cell that is characteristic in tuberculosis lesions and made great contributions to our knowledge of how the body builds resistance to tuberculosis. She was the first woman ever elected to the National Academy of Sciences. And Josephine Roche (*above, right*) became president of the Rocky Mountain Fuel Company in 1929 and subsequently served three years as Assistant Secretary of the U. S. Treasury. At the right is Annette Adams of San Francisco, who in the early nineteen-twenties was for a time Assistant Attorney General of the United States. This picture of her, taken early in her prosecuting career, suggests how many women, before 1920, felt they must look as much as possible like men to succeed in a profession dominated by men; that idea pretty well dissolved in the nineteen-twenties.

During the nineteen-twenties women not only forged ahead in occupations which were traditional, for men if not for women, but also developed new occupations, and even to old ones added something new. At the left is a librarian counseling a child on her reading, at the Muhlenberg Branch of the New York Public Library; below is a museum worker explaining works of art to a group of children. Both these women were taking advantage of a new impulse which flowered in the progressive education movement—the impulse to seize upon the natural interest of children in literature and art, and instead of straight-jacketing it by formal discipline, to help the children follow their own tastes through the gentlest of guidance. It would seem that both of these women were good at their jobs, to judge from the concentration displayed by the children in the two photographs.

The expanding twenties saw an enormous growth in advertising agencies; and, especially in those offices which handled women's accounts, there were golden opportunities for women in executive positions. Mrs. Stanley Resor and Miss Ruth Waldo of J. Walter Thompson are only two of a number of women who became highly successful in this field. Women's fashions offered another avenue; Mrs. Edna Woolman Chase, editor of *Vogue*, became a real power in the fashion world, and she was followed by Carmel Snow, who graduated from the *Vogue* school to become editor of *Harper's Bazaar*. On the staffs of both magazines, there was room for ambitious girls with style sense. Moreover, the executive offices of the great department stores were opening their doors more and more to women (we've already mentioned Dorothy Shaver's signal success). Paris still set the styles, but as time went on American women began to win their spurs as designers. Below is one of them—Elizabeth Hawes, who, on graduating from Vassar in 1925, served an apprenticeship in several New York shops, studied design in Paris, and opened her own establishment in 1928. Presumably, Miss Hawes does not customarily work with quite so many scissors and tape-measures as appear here.

A particularly gaudy flower of the nineteen-twenties was Mary Louise Cecelia Guinan, better known as Texas Guinan, who after a varied career as circus rider, chorus girl, vaudeville trouper, and movie actress, became in her middle age the queen of the New York night clubs—in partnership with one Larry Fay, an ex-taxi-driver who had muscled into control of a sector of the New York taxi business and was later to be a racketeer in the milk industry. Texas Guinan had a contagiously hearty manner—her favorite greeting was "Hello, sucker!"—and when she presided over a night club she made the consumers of illicit liquor (remember, this was during prohibition) feel and act boisterously at home. She appears above in her role of Queen of the Night Club, in a Warner Brothers movie; at the right, above, she is allegedly signing a contract to appear in another show, *The Padlocks of 1927*—the correct procedure in contract-signing apparently being to wear riding clothes and sit on a desk which has been moved to an exposed position on a terrace, while Mr. C. William Morganstern is occupied in keeping the documents from blowing away.

Of perplexing interest to future sociologists will be another occupation that began its flourishing life during the late twenties—that of drum-majorette. The correct strut is here being demonstrated at a convention of the Dancing Masters of America by Miss Mildred Bryan of Wilmington, Delaware, who succeeds in conveying an effect which is one part military, several parts anatomical.

It's curious how many women have a weakness for fortune-tellers—and how many fortune-tellers are women. The one above is using both playing cards and palmistry to reveal the future of the lady in the large hat. The two women below are attempting to establish contact with the spirit world and this early experiment in spirit photography shows, by some means or other, the ghostly shape of a gentleman with a mustache to the right of them and above.

Of the mediums who challenged the skepticism of students of spiritualism, none aroused a greater furor during the nineteen-twenties than "Margery," otherwise Mrs. L. R. G. Crandon of Boston, who could arrange her guests in a circle, make them hold one another's hands, and then, after the room had been darkened, ingeniously "materialize" ghostly luminous shapes before them. Her "spirit guide" was named Walter.

The nineteen-twenties witnessed also the arrival of the policewoman. When New York City organized the Bureau of Policewomen in April 1926 its members were found useful in looking after women and children who were prisoners or suspects, doing detective work on shoplifting, and performing other special duties. Above you see former Police Commissioner Edward P. Mulrooney of New York and Mary Sullivan, onetime head of the Policewoman's Bureau, whose cheerful countenance gives the lie to W. S. Gilbert's immortal line, "A policeman's lot is not a happy one." In the mid-forties, Miss Sullivan had her own radio program, "Mary Sullivan, Policewoman." During World War II the manpower shortage increased the demand for policewomen for other duties. At the right, Mrs. Artie Stockdale and Mrs. Ann Bennett are reporting for traffic duty in Indianapolis in 1943; below, four Detroit policewomen are engaged in businesslike target practice in 1942.

As for the oldest profession of all, it continued to offer the easiest way for many women, despite legal prohibition, the break-up of prostitution rings, and, as time went on, what might be described as amateur competition. The Lynds in their admirable social study, *Middletown*, referring to this subject, report an estimated twenty-five houses of prostitution in 1890 as compared with two or three in 1929 (after a state act was passed in 1915 which drove the institution underground), adding; ". . . but a comparison with 1890 on this point is fruitless, because, as the judge of the juvenile court points out, 'the automobile has become a house of prostitution on wheels.'" On this page appear two scenes from Eugene Walter's successful play, *The Easiest Way*, which stirred furious controversy on its appearance in 1909, with lovely Frances Starr in the lead, because it dragged into the open a subject considered unmentionable. In the upper picture the heroine is repudiating her ill-gotten luxury for the pure love of a fine young man, but in the lower picture she finds the path of virtue offers very slim pickings.

Despite the increase in the number and variety of feminine salary-earners and wage-earners, the great majority of American women continued to lead the domestic life—which among several million farm women included all manner of farming duties. Here is a cheerful member of this large group, Mrs. Emery Forbes of Peoria County, Illinois, with her pet pig, Oscar. The picture dates from 1942; a generation earlier her costume would probably have been much less convenient.

The huge and uninterrupted growth of governments—local, state, and particularly federal—
during the past fifty years has developed all manner of new occupations for women. Above,
for example, is a home demonstration agent of the Department of Agriculture, calling on
a farm wife in the San Joaquin Valley in California—advising her, possibly, on family
financial planning, or on kitchen arrangement, or on gardening, or on making, washing, and
mending clothes, or on washing a cream separator. During a single recent year such home
demonstration agents—working as part of an Extension Service financed partly by the U. S.
Department of Agriculture, partly by states, counties, and land-grant colleges—made nearly
a million home visits and gave nearly a quarter million demonstrations of homemaking
methods attended by three and three quarter million women.

THE LITTLE ONES

In the mid-nineties, when children were still supposed to be seen and not heard, proud mothers went to considerable pains to make them worth looking at. How brilliantly at least one of them succeeded is demonstrated by the very young lady above dressed in her finest. Nothing was spared: velvet, lace, fur, satin ribbon, ruchings, and ostrich feathers were artfully combined into this costume of infinite, if miniature, splendor. The drawing of the little girl's dress is simpler, but not exactly plain, and the fine suit at the right, despite the skirt, is for a little boy.

An article in the August 1896 issue of the *Queen of Fashion*, called "Chats With Young Mothers," begins firmly, "One of the earliest lessons a child has to learn is obedience. Once a child is taught to obey, all other good habits come comparatively easily. Make no unreasonable demands, but see that you are obeyed." The author continues, more mildly, to stress the importance of contentment, explaining that the child must early learn to keep itself happily occupied. "Nothing is more disagreeable than a whining child," she adds. Here is revealed, quite clearly, the ideal of a household which was run, first of all, for the comfort of the older members, together with a strong sense that the habit of obedience or discipline in the children was going to make life more agreeable for everybody. The children on this page were brought up in this school of thought. The photograph above was made in 1892, that at the upper right in 1894, and the lower one in 1887. It is too early to see if the habit of obedience has wholly warped their natures; the little boy in the center above clearly has doubts about something, but the one-year-old in the upper right displays a serene optimism that may be due more to her white, fur-trimmed silk coat than to her confidence in the manner of her upbringing. It was not until the nineteen-twenties that the regime of strict discipline was generally replaced by a totally different concept in the training of children. By that time, the idea became paramount that the child's personality must not be repressed, lest dreadful things develop in later life.

This is the way children were dressed to have their pictures taken at the turn of the century and shortly thereafter. The two flower-girls above seem more apprehensive than wedding attendants should appear; the high button shoes on the girl at the upper right appear unduly sensible in contrast to her frivolous frilled hat; the boy below is indeed the pattern of negligent elegance; the young lady at the right, below, has mounted a footstool, the better to pose thoughtfully on the back of a chair. It will be seen that these pictures were made before the advent of the ubiquitous smile.

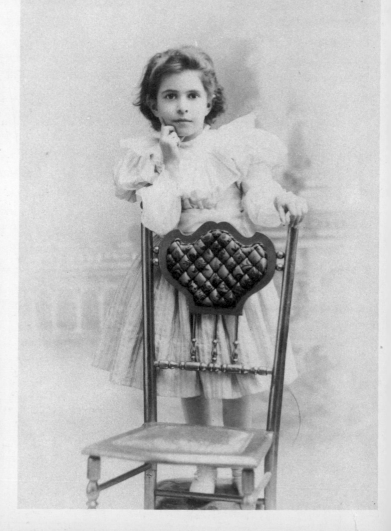

CHAPTER I.

PLAYING PILGRIMS.

"CHRISTMAS won't be Christmas without any presents," grumbled Jo, lying on the rug.

"It's so dreadful to be poor!" sighed Meg, looking down at her old dress.

"I don't think it's fair for some girls to have lots of pretty things, and other girls nothing at all," added little Amy, with an injured sniff.

"We've got father and mother, and each other, anyhow," said Beth, contentedly, from her corner.

The four young faces on which the firelight shone brightened at the cheerful words, but darkened again as Jo said sadly,—

CHAPTER FIRST

"I never saw an eye so bright,
 And yet so soft as hers;
It sometimes swam in liquid light,
 And sometimes swam in tears;
It seemed a beauty set apart
 For softness and for sighs."

    —Mrs. Welby.

THE school-room at Roselands was a very pleasant apartment; the ceiling, it is true, was somewhat lower than in the more modern portion of the building, for the wing in which it was situated dated back to the old-fashioned days prior to the Revolution, while the larger part of the mansion had not stood more than twenty or thirty years; but the effect was relieved by windows reaching from floor to ceil-

These students of the Glen Ridge, New Jersey, primary school have been studying the habits of the American Indians. This explains the cryptic message on the blackboard, "all of the men took a puff," which referred to a pipe of peace. The pages above are opening chapters of two books widely read among the girls of the class —*Little Women* and *Elsie Dinsmore*. And let those mothers of today who worry unduly about the horrors of the comic strip and the more sensational movies their children are exposed to, reflect that the horrendous illustration at the left (from "Soria Moria Castle" in the *Red Fairy Book*) was standard pictorial fare for the little ones of the Age of Innocence.

A family as handsome—and as exquisitely attired—as this one brought out the best efforts of a fashionable photographer in the early twentieth century. This picture was made in London when the American family portrayed was on one of its annual European visits. That is a little boy standing by his mother's knee, despite the lacy dress, and it was considered especially romantic to have him barefoot.

There were—and are—conflicting schools of thought about exact procedure in the bringing up of children, but in recent years there has been general agreement that patterns of child behavior are of the greatest importance. In the nursery school at Vassar, where these pictures were taken, students are making careful notes on the play-habits and work-habits of the very young. The young artist may be slightly hampered by having to stand on tip-toe to reach the very top of her canvas but you may be sure that no one will do anything but admire the finished product as an untrammeled bit of pure self-expression.

Nor are the benefits of advanced theories of child development limited to the few who are financially well off. Children of migrant farm laborers are provided with scientifically prepared toys and books, and are offered the same basic opportunities to "learn by doing" that the children of the wealthy in private nursery schools have. The lower photograph shows a group of very small children enjoying the delights of literature while the little girls above are absorbed in pretending to iron a dress. Both pictures were taken near Yakima, Washington, in 1941 at a migratory labor camp run by the Farm Security Administration.

"It's broccoli, dear."
"I say it's spinach, and I say the hell with it."

It must be admitted that there are times when even the most devoted mothers, and those most conscientiously committed to the idea of free expression for their children, are somewhat taken aback and even defeated by the results. Carl Rose's famous cartoon above, which appeared in *The New Yorker* for December 8, 1928, and his spirited drawing below, from *The New Yorker* of June 11, 1927, struck responsive chords in thousands of young parents.

The photograph below shows a "six-year-old bundle of personality" winning a prize in a Los Angeles Junior Pageant. There is a large section of the American public that takes what seems to those outside it a perverted delight in seeing children copying certain music-hall antics of their elders. The six-year-old torch singer, drum majorette, and adagio dancer are curious products of this aberration, not to mention baby parades.

"Precious—shall mother be cross?"

A FEW CHAMPIONS

Just in case anyone should fall into the error of assuming that sports champions run true to type, let us consider a few women of prowess in sport who bear small resemblance to one another. On this page you see two photographs of Annette Kellerman, whose success as a swimming champion was only the springboard for her many other activities. As a movie star she appeared in *Neptune's Daughter* and then (in 1916) in the spectacular Fox production, *Daughter of the Gods,* the making of which involved such operations as remaking part of the island of Jamaica, building a Moorish city there, importing a troupe of camels, and restoring a ruined Spanish fort. She gave her name to the one-piece jersey bathing suit —a most revolutionary garment—that was generally worn under a modest black taffetta affair by non-champion bathers in the twenties. Her celebrated figure, silhouetted at the right, looks a little odd by present-day standards.

By the mid-twenties Annette Kellerman was spreading the doctrine of "Universal Health" throughout Europe. In Germany, Denmark, Sweden, France, and Spain, she demonstrated her exercises and lectured in the language of the country. A press release of 1927 (when the photograph at the left was taken) said, "Miss Kellerman holds the stage twenty minutes alone in the Gym scene and seems to have no difficulty at all in talking the different languages and doing the exercises at the same time." With dancing, singing, wire walking, diving, and various foreign tongues at her command, she was equipped for almost any situation.

On August 6, 1926, Gertrude Ederle swam the English Channel in fourteen and a half hours. She was not only the first woman ever to accomplish this feat; she bettered by almost two hours the time of the fastest of the five men who had done it. She is shown at the left in the course of her classic swim. In the picture below, Gertrude Ederle, some thirteen years later, appears with another aquatic star, Eleanor Holm. Both girls are preparing for another kind of endurance test—Billy Rose's Aquacade at the World's Fair in New York in 1939.

The amateur champion who reaps no financial reward from her victories is here represented by Glenna Collett, who started playing tournament golf in 1918 when she was only fifteen. She was six times national woman's champion between the years 1922 and 1935. You see her below in 1923, wearing the tweed skirt and sweater which she, with Joyce Wethered, inaugurated as standard clothes for golf.

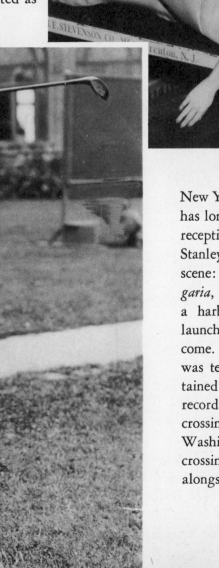

New York's fashion of welcoming distinguished visitors has long been a byword, but the first really spectacular reception was for Gertrude Ederle on August 27, 1926. Stanley Walker, in *Mrs. Astor's Horse*, describes the scene: "Down the bay two airplanes circled the *Berengaria*, two hydroplanes skimmed along the water, and a harbor full of tugs, excursion steamers, cutters, launches, motor boats, and sailboats joined in the welcome. Those having whistles tied them down. The din was terrific." Mayor Walker's welcoming speech contained the following ringing passage: "When history records the great crossings, they will speak of Moses crossing the Red Sea, Caesar crossing the Rubicon, and Washington crossing the Delaware, but frankly, your crossing of the British Channel must take its place alongside of these."

Helen Wills is the shining example of the amateur sports champion who is so dedicated to the serious business of winning that her whole life centers in her game. She appears above in the course of defeating Kay Stammers of England (with her customary score of 6-2, 6-1) in the quarter-finals of the Wimbledon Tournament, June 28, 1938. She won the Wimbledon singles championship seven times from 1927 to 1938—every year she played.

Helen Wills on the courts in 1921 (*above*); in 1938 (*below*); and in 1942 (*right*).

Helen Wills' score board in the *Encyclopedia of Sports* is awe-inspiring. Beginning at fifteen, when she won the national girls' championship at Forest Hills (see previous page) and continuing until she won the women's singles at Wimbledon in 1938, she piled up a series of victories that was indeed formidable. She was seven times U.S.A. singles champion; three times U.S.A. doubles champion; U.S.A. mixed doubles champion twice; French singles champion four times; and she won ten times at Wimbledon—twice in doubles, the rest in singles. In 1936, she and Howard Kinsey volleyed a ball for 78 minutes, hitting the ball 2001 times without a miss. They could have gone on, but Kinsey had to stop to give a lesson. In her long career of tournament tennis, Helen Wills was seldom defeated. Molla Mallory beat her when she first tried for the women's championship at the age of 16, but she won the title from that seasoned player the following year (in 1923). The photographs on this page were taken in Cannes in 1926 when the young Helen came up against the great French player, Suzanne Lenglen—and very nearly beat her. They are standing together at the left, and the upper picture, showing people who couldn't get tickets and stood on ladders to watch the match, shows the interest this event aroused.

Let it never be said that the more hazardous occupations are for men only. Bee Kyle, shown below in mid-air, earned her living by diving from a great height into a small tank. Annie Edson Taylor on October 24, 1901 (her 43rd birthday), spent 35 rough minutes going over Niagara Falls in a barrel. You see her with the barrel, in the very costume she wore during her experiment perilous.

Mountain climbing as a sport appeals to nearly as many wome[n] as men according to the membership figures of organization[s] of American climbers. The Appalachian Mountain Club, th[e] Sierra Club, and The Mountaineers—representing Massachu[setts], California, and Washington, respectively—report an equa[l] number of women and men members. Mazamas (in Oregon[)] and the Colorado Mountain Club have more men than wome[n,] but they all agree that their women members include man[y] fine climbers. Georgia Engelhard, below, has a distinguishe[d] reputation in mountaineering circles and has to her cred[it] many first ascents in the Canadian Rockies.

DANGER AND DARING

An early mountaineer was Annie Smith Peck, shown above in the costume in which she ascended the Matterhorn in 1895 (it was harder then). She was the first woman to climb Orizaba (1897), and she conquered numerous majestic peaks in South America. She also taught Latin at Smith College.

The Flying Behees (*left*) are current stars of the circus. An earlier star was Bird Millman, seated above on the wire on which she danced, turned somersaults, and once, in 1924, crossed lower Broadway twenty-five stories above the ground. Mabel Cody (*below*) is changing vehicles in mid-slipstream —from car to plane at Daytona Beach in 1927.

The picture above shows Amelia Earhart landing in Ireland; the lower one shows her landing in New York in 1928.

The two pictures on the opposite page mark two milestones in Amelia Earhart's early career; they also mark two milestones in aviation. When she flew the Atlantic in 1928 with Wilmer Stutz and Louis Gordon she was the first woman to do so, and New York welcomed her back with ceremonies befitting the importance of her accomplishment. In the photograph, Acting Mayor Joseph McKee is decorating her with the city's medal while her flying companions stand by, to the right. The upper picture was taken just after she had landed in Ireland after her transatlantic solo flight of May 20, 1932—another feat she was the first woman to perform. The photograph below is a sad one. It was taken on March 12, 1937, when Amelia Earhart, then Mrs. George Palmer Putnam, was inspecting her big Lockheed Electra, three days before she took off for the round-the-world flight on which she was lost.

In 1929 Anne Morrow, the daughter of Dwight Morrow, a partner in J. P. Morgan & Co. and Ambassador to Mexico, became one of the most envied girls in the United States by marrying the country's top hero—Charles A. Lindbergh, who two years before had made the first solo flight across the Atlantic. Mrs. Lindbergh learned to operate a plane and a radio and became a working partner with her famous husband on long exploratory flights. Mrs. Lindbergh's skill as a flyer is most likely the result of her husband's tutoring, but no one but herself is responsible for her skill in writing. Her *North to the Orient* (1935) and *Listen, the Wind* (1938) established her as a master of sensitive, beautiful prose. The photograph at the left shows the Lindberghs in 1933 arriving at Woolston, near Southampton, England. The one below shows Mrs. Lindbergh in October 1947, on her return from Europe.

In these air-minded times when women and girls learn to fly without anybody's making any great to-do over it, it is hard to remember how truly hazardous flying was in the fragile, unstable planes of the early days. Ruth Law, whose picture appears on page 83 of this book, was one of the seven American licensed women flyers before World War I. The first of this hardy group was Harriet Quimby, who was the first woman to fly the English Channel, and who was killed at the Boston Aviation Meet in July 1912, less than a year from the time she won her license. Julia Clark, another one of the group, was killed in June 1912 at the State Fair Grounds in Springfield, Illinois, when her plane crashed in an exhibition flight. The others, however—Mathilda Moisant, Blanche Scott, and Katherine and Marjorie Stinson—survived the very real dangers of pioneer aviation.

Delia Akeley was a co-worker with her husband, Carl E. Akele on numerous scientific expeditions in Africa between 1905 an 1911 and assisted him in the construction of his famous habit groups of animals. Obviously the elephant must be killed be fore he can be mounted, and here is Mrs. Akeley perched upo the first one that she killed. She made two African expeditio alone for the Brooklyn Museum in the twenties and discovere new species of antelopes and birds.

Mary Hastings Bradley thought her lion was dead when the picture was snapped. Actually he was beginning to revive, as the opening eyes show. (He was dispatched shortly afterward with no harm to the hunter.) Mrs. Bradley's explorations have taken her into the gorilla country of the Belgian Congo, the tiger regions of Indo-China and Sumatra, and among the Pygmies of Africa, and have won for her a solid reputation among scientists. She is a Fellow of the Royal Geographical Society.

Mrs. William Harkness does not appear to be in any particular danger from the baby giant panda she is attempting to feed with a spoon. The dangers and hardships came with the expedition to capture the beguiling creature. This is the second panda Mrs. Harkness brought to the United States. The photograph was taken in November 1938.

Mabel Stark (*above*) began her career as the "World's Only Woman Tiger Trainer" when she was a trained nurse on vacation and visited the winter quarters of the Barnes Circus. She went into a tiger's cage on a dare, liked it, and never went back to the hospital. Ethel Purtle entered show business through matrimony. Her husband, a motorcyclist, happened to have a lion, and Mrs. Purtle originated the alarming act in which she and King tear around the wooden bowl of Purtle's Motordrome in a midget racing car.

MANNERS AND CUSTOMS

Arthur M. Schlesinger in his charming and perceptive little history of American books of etiquette—*Learning How to Behave*—lists certain conditions in the early days of this country that accounted for the rash of such books that have appeared from Colonial days to the present time. First, the first settlers did not in the main come from the best society; second, there was no native hereditary society here to set a standard of behavior; third, the business of carving a life out of a wilderness left little time to cultivate manners; fourth, women, who in Western Europe had greatly outnumbered men and had been the strict guardians of propriety, were in the minority in the New World. However, the desire to behave properly was strong, and manuals that professed to teach one to behave were in great demand, and Mr. Schlesinger concludes the introduction to his book with these kindly words: "The account has its mirthful moments, but the reader who smiles should smile with compassion, for he is witnessing one aspect of the common man's struggle to achieve a larger degree of human dignity and self-respect."

The two pictures on this page illustrate the extreme decorum that characterized polite behavior in nineteenth-century America. The upper group are spending a quiet Sunday afternoon in New York's Central Park; the rural couple at the right, in John George Brown's painting, "The Old Stile," are doing the same thing in the country.

Perhaps nothing illustrates more clearly the shift in emphasis on outward forms that has been going on in recent years than the changing conventions of mourning. The traditional forms remain: the conventional periods of wearing black for husband, mother, father, son, or daughter are longer than for grandparents, aunts and uncles, sisters and brothers (although these periods are shorter than formerly); correct mourning still precludes the wearing of glossy materials, jewelry with colored stones, patent leather shoes, and hats of shiny black straw; black-bordered writing paper and handkerchiefs are still obtainable. But these outward and visible signs are no longer mandatory. The convention of mourning remains for those who wish to follow it; but there is no criticism attached to the woman who appears in her customary clothes the day after the funeral, and the sight of a woman dressed in deep mourning is increasingly rare. It has been some time since shops advertised mourning clothes; the illustration below, from the catalogue of Franklin Simon and Company, dates from 1921. The photograph shows a widow in customary attire in the nineties.

Dignity and Distinction in Black and White Gowns

Of Crepe de Chine or Canton Silk Crepe, for Mourning Wear.   Smart Hats

Black and White Shop—Fifth Floor

The Martha Washington Hotel in New York (for women only) was established in 1903 for the peace of mind of nervous ladies who slept better if they knew there wasn't a strange man in the next room. As you see at the right, the employees also were women. Sometimes the hotels were nervous, too, and a woman traveling alone in the nineties was often refused admission unless she had a note of introduction. As late as 1907, Mrs. Harriot Stanton Blatch, a prominent suffragist, sued the Hoffman House in New York because the hotel declined to serve her dinner on the roof-garden, where she had arrived, unescorted, after six o'clock in the evening.

John Sloan's spirited painting, "Dust Storm, Fifth Avenue," shows New York's Flatiron Building in 1906. This corner of 23rd Street and Fifth Avenue was exceedingly windy and men of low minds would loiter there on breezy days when the wind revealed more of the young ladies than their costumes were intended to permit.

"The Cruise of the New York Yacht Club—A Pleasant Evening in Harbor" is the title of the drawing above by T. de Thulstrup which appeared in the August 19, 1899, issue of *Harper's Weekly*. Do not leap to the conclusion that the yachtsman seated on the deck is somebody's father. Beards were worn by quite young men in the nineties. The chaperone is not visible, but you may be sure she is near by.

"For the Colonel's lady and Judy O'Grady are sisters, under their skins"

Irving Berlin's "Alexander's Rag-time Band" (1911), according to Alexander Woollcott, "set the shoulders of America swinging with syncopated jubilance" and ushered in a tremendous vogue for a new kind of dancing that horrified the strait-laced. The "Turkey Trot," the "Bunny Hug," and other dances were possibly more vigorous than graceful, but those who engaged in them found them very good fun, despite such critics as Walter Tittle, whose drawing above appeared in *Harper's Weekly* in 1912. Eleven years later, the rowdiness of these dances had smoothed down to the Fox-trot, but a new misdemeanor at dances was engaging the attention of the old guard—the practice of applying make-up in public between dances. The drawing below, by Helen Dryden, is from the January 1, 1923, issue of *Vogue*.

Only three decades from the Age of Innocence to This Freedom. Every one is so engagingly frank —nothing is concealed— ladies restore their complexions at the table between each fox-trot, and "make it snappy" is the last word

It is fitting, if unexpected, to discover that John Murray Anderson, the theatrical and motion picture director, who has written, devised, and staged more than forty musical comedies, should himself be a past master of the dance. He is here shown, with his partner, in a striking pose during the dance mania that convulsed the country in the years 1912-17.

The Tango and the Maxixe (demonstrated by Mr. and Mrs. John Murray Anderson) are illustrated above, as they were performed in 1914. The trousers worn by Mrs. Anderson reflect a style adopted by some women as suitable for the strenuous dances of this period. The nineteen-twenties, which were marked by considerable intemperance in other directions, were moderate (compared with the decades that preceded and followed them) in the matter of dancing, despite the brief vogue of the Charleston. The lower picture, taken in January 1938, shows swing addicts in the Paramount Theatre, so carried away by Benny Goodman's music that they swarmed on the stage and put on an impromptu act.

"The Dance-Mad Younger Set" is the title of the above drawing by John Held, Jr., and it appeared in the April 28, 1927, issue of *Life*. Granted that Mr. Held was a cartoonist and not a photographer, nevertheless the implications of his drawings were close enough to reality to convey something of the panic that seized upon parents of young girls in the twenties (parents who themselves had grown up with the quiet pleasures illustrated on page 146) when they saw their daughters caught up in the undoubted revolution in manners that marked the "Jazz Age," whose foremost reporter was F. Scott Fitzgerald. Have you read *This Side of Paradise* lately?

Frederick Lewis Allen, in his history of the nineteen-twenties, *Only Yesterday,* lists as influences in the revolution in manners and morals of the period, post-war disillusion, the new status of women, the Freudian gospel that sex repression was the cause of many ills, the closed automobile, prohibition, the sex and confession magazines, and the movies. "Each of them as an influence," Mr. Allen writes, "was played upon by all the others; none of them could alone have changed to any great degree the folkways of America; together their force was irresistible." Various forces attempted to halt what they considered the downhill headlong progress of the younger generation: the church, women's clubs, teachers, and, most notably, the woman shown above in the black feathered hat—Mrs. Emily Post, who in her *Etiquette, The Blue Book of Social Usage,* appearing first in 1922, fought hard, as Mr. Schlesinger puts it, "to preserve the punctilious standards of her own heritage." But even Mrs. Post failed, and in subsequent editions of her book amended many of her earlier dicta. The John Held, Jr., drawing below appeared in *Life,* October 29, 1925.

Ursula: IS MY NOSE SHINY, DEARIE?
Lambert: NO, BUT YOUR RIGHT KNEE IS DUSTY.

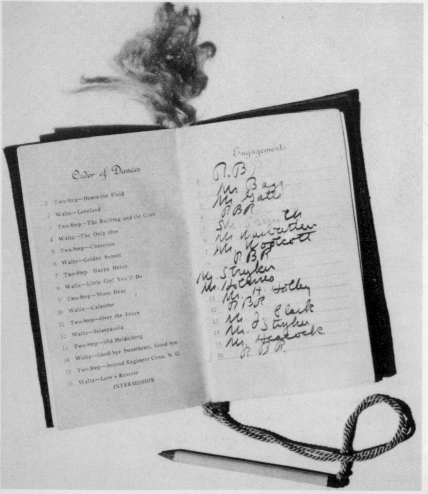

Order of Dances

1 Two-Step—Down the Field
2 Waltz—Loveland
3 Two-Step—The Bullfrog and the Coon
4 Waltz—The Only One
5 Two-Step—Cheyenne
6 Waltz—Golden Sunset
7 Two-Step—Happy Heine
8 Waltz—Little Girl You'll Do
9 Two-Step—Moon Dear
10 Waltz—Calanthe
11 Two-Step—Over the Fence
12 Waltz—Solaspanola
13 Two-Step—Old Heidelberg
14 Waltz—Good-bye Sweetheart, Good-bye
15 Two-Step—Second Regiment Conn. N. G.
16 Waltz—Love's Reverie
INTERMISSION

Engagements

The photograph above has captured a moment in the progress of a dance given at the Ypsilanti Normal School some time before the year 1910. Very likely the first remark of many of these men was, "Do you reverse?" *Hill's Manual,* that hardy perennial among guides to behavior, as late as 1918 began the section on "Etiquette of the Party and Ball" with the following ominous words, ". . . we will not express an opinion concerning the propriety or the impropriety of dancing. In the simple act of passing through the figures of the dance there need be no wrong committed; but as the ball is often conducted, very serious and unfortunate results follow. . . . Well may the watchful parent look with anxiety and suspicion upon the ball, because its associations are so frequently dangerous."

The dance card at the left dates from 1906, when it recorded the engagements of a young lady at the Hamilton College Senior Ball in June. The Mr. Stryker who was listed for two dances is a distinguished trial lawyer and author; the partner for No. 7, "Two-Step—Happy Heine," was the late Alexander Woollcott (with his name misspelled).

The social climate of the thirties differed somewhat from that of the preceding decade. The revolution against the Puritan tradition, at least in its most public demonstrations, had reached its zenith in the late twenties, and the sobering effects of the Depression were reflected in a far more serious attitude toward marriage and the family. As Frederick Lewis Allen puts it in *Since Yesterday*, "Not that there was any measurable increase in abstinence, continence, or modesty. . . . Yet in the country at large there was a change of mood, a change of emphasis." One facet of the reaction against the general whoop-la of the twenties was a return to formal clothes for evening parties. The photograph above, taken at a Vassar Prom in the mid-thirties, shows the men in tails—a costume that had all but disappeared, among younger men at least, during the relaxed atmosphere of the twenties.

In 1900 Olga Nethersole caused a tremendous furore when she appeared in Clyde Fitch's dramatic version of Daudet's *Sapho.* The famous scene in which she was carried up a circular staircase to what Thomas Beer called "a theoretic bedroom" was so disturbing to the guardians of public morals that Miss Nethersole was arrested. The photograph at the left shows her in the costume of Emmy Legrant (the heroine of *Sapho*), smoking a cigarette—obviously a courtesan! The moral turpitude formerly associated with the use of tobacco is hard for young people of today to realize; equally hard to comprehend is the strong prejudice that once existed against men smoking in the presence of women. "We think the prospects for the future happiness of that young girl are small, who will be seen in public with a gentleman who is smoking," was the decision of one writer on etiquette in 1891, and President McKinley would not permit a photograph to be made of him with a cigar. "We must not let the young men of this country see their President smoking," he declared.

The very idea of women smoking was termed "a horror and a crying shame" in 1898 by a writer on etiquette, who, however, admitted that the dreadful habit, recently introduced from Europe, had been taken up by a few Americans. At any rate, smoking among American women was rare before World War I. Once they began, there was no stopping them. Estimates from *Moody's Investor's Survey, Printer's Ink,* and the Milwaukee *Journal* provide the following statistics: women smokers accounted for about 5 per cent of the cigarette consumption in 1923, 17 per cent in 1934, 29 per cent in 1944, and 38 per cent in 1948. Yet prejudice remained so strong in certain quarters that tobacco manufacturers were for a long time very cautious about advertisements that showed women actually smoking. The first Lucky Strike advertisement showing a woman with a cigarette appeared in May 1932; the one at the right dates from June 1934.

The W.C.T.U., under the able leadership of Frances Willard, exerted a powerful influence and undoubtedly aided greatly in the wave of prohibitory legislation which began in 1907 (the year the advertisement above appeared in *Harper's Weekly*). By 1919, thirty-three states had prohibited the liquor traffic, and the 18th Amendment was swept into the laws of the country on January 16, 1920.

Carry Amelia Moore Nation, who appears above with her celebrated hatchet and at the right snatching a cigarette from the offending lips of a little boy, was a colorful figure in the temperance movement. She was born in Kentucky in 1846 of a mother who spent her last years in an insane asylum, under the delusion that she was Queen Victoria. Mrs. Nation, believing that she was divinely appointed to destroy the saloon, began her career of demolition in Kansas in 1899. It was already a dry state, and she first directed her operations against illicit barrooms. Later she widened her orbit to include the entire country, and was in jail more than twenty-five times because of her vigorous destruction of bottles and barrels, fixtures and mirrors.

As far back as 1873 a group of women in Hillsboro, Ohio, gathered for prayer, then marched two by two to the saloons of the town, appealing to the saloon keepers to give up their business. This was the beginning of the Woman's Crusade against the demon rum, which lasted only six months but had meanwhile spread all over the country. The next year the Woman's Christian Temperance Union was founded.

It is only fair to assume that no one was more surprised by the more violent by-products of Prohibition than the high-minded prohibitionists. That they expected a reign of lawlessness, amounting in certain areas to a reign of terror as gangsters fought gangsters with sub-machine guns, rumrunners fought running battles with revenue agents, and otherwise law-abiding citizens broke this particular law daily, is impossible to believe. The country had adopted the new amendment willingly, but as time went on it became apparent that many Americans thought that Prohibition was a fine thing—for other people. The speakeasy and the bootlegger grew up overnight. And still more significant was the increase in mixed drinking, which was so widespread that by the time prohibition ended, what had once been saloons for men only, became, almost universally, bars patronized by both sexes together. Drinking by women had increased incalculably.

Two cartoons of the twenties are shown here. The one at the right, "The Woman Who Cut Her Husband's Bootlegger," by Rea Irvin, appeared in the November 7, 1925, issue of *The New Yorker*, and the one below, by John Held, Jr., was published by *Liberty*, February 27, 1932.

The Evening *Moderne*—Mixing and blending the bathtub gin

The cocktail party, illustrated by Guy Pène du Bois's painting below, emerged in the era of Prohibition as a recognized form of entertainment, so widespread was open defiance of the 18th Amendment. Another phenomenon of the period was the speakeasy, where men and women gathered in varying degrees of bibulous congeniality. Elmer Davis wrote, "The old days when father spent his evenings at Cassidy's bar with the rest of the boys are gone, and probably forever; Cassidy may still be in business at the old stand and father may still go down there of evenings, but since prohibition mother goes down with him." The speakeasy as such ranged from a waterfront dive, where the worst sort of near-poison was sold, to an elegant establishment which had the atmosphere of a good club and served the best food in town. It was only in New York, to be sure, that the latter type really flourished. In other parts of the country, people who wanted to drink in safety—reports of severe illness, blindness, and even death from bad liquor were only too common—were more likely to depend on a reliable boot-legger for their whiskey and gin (or the alcohol from which they made their own gin).

IMPORTED

Distinguished English arrivals that present the case when a case in the hand is worth two, two miles out, or on top of a truck, or well, you finish it, bottoms up. P.S.— An exclusive story, from London to Saks-Fifth Avenue.

A capacious case for that precocious Sundae School class of Elinor Wylie's (see New Yorker, Feb. 19.) English cowhide case, with two metal quart flasks, shaker, four cups (right). 48.50

A dandy brief case surprise! Of fine London cowhide, it holds three glass flasks, and the case has double locks. 34.50. (Above)

Always invited to go on the pleasantest voyages — traveling case with everything you want, i. e., shaker, vacuum ice bottle, 2 nickel and glass bottles, 6 cups. Cowhide case, suede lined. 85.00.

The popular big brother to the powder compact is the refreshment compact — a folding shaker, 4 cups, squeezer, sugar box; all fit neatly into a cowhide case. 12.50.

We furnish the case—you furnish the fun! And what a case! Handsome black cowhide, sumptuously outfitted in sterling silver — two quart flasks, 8 cups, quart shaker. 375.00—and worth it!

LEATHER GOODS DEPARTMENT—STREET FLOOR

SAKS — FIFTH AVENUE

FORTY-NINTH to FIFTIETH STREET

Wide public approval was back of the above advertisement which appeared in *The New Yorker*, March 6, 1926—a day when you carried your own.

Many people believe that women were largely responsible for Prohibition. Certainly the early temperance movement didn't get much of anywhere until the women joined it. And, strangely enough, it was women who were largely responsible for repeal. Mrs. Charles Sabin (*seated, below*) organized the most militant of the forces for repeal, the Women's Organization for Prohibition Reform, in 1929. (By December 1933 the country was wet again.) To another woman, Mabel Walker Willebrandt (*right*), Assistant Attorney General of the U. S., was given the important, impossible job of enforcing Prohibition.

About 1891

Probably taken after the trial

MISS LIZZIE BORDEN

On Thursday, August 4, 1892, a particularly shocking double murder rocked the town of Fall River, Massachusetts. A respected citizen of the town, one Mr. Borden, and his wife were discovered hacked almost to pieces. Lizzie Borden, a daughter of the house, was suspected, arrested, and tried for the crime. She was not convicted, but a popular song of the time shows the popular sentiment:

> "Lizzie Borden took an axe,
> Gave her father forty whacks.
> When she saw what she had done,
> She gave her mother forty-one."

One often hears amateur students of crime sigh for the old days when the country would be stirred from coast to coast over a particularly hair-raising murder. These critics complain that crimes today haven't the picturesque quality or the epic proportions of those of an earlier time. On this page and the next we show some of the principals of a few of the classic crimes of the past fifty years. It is quite true that they appear to lose in stature as they approach the present, but let us remember that now the newspapers are full of far more shattering tragedies almost daily, in all parts of a troubled world, and that murders, while they unfortunately still go on, are unlikely therefore to command the sustained interest they once did.

The Thaw case was no mystery. On the night of June 25, 1906, a large part of the audience on the roof of Madison Square Garden in New York saw Harry Kendall Thaw draw a revolver and shoot the noted architect, Stanford White, three times in the head, killing him instantly. It was the evidence that came out during Thaw's trial and the newspaper accounts of the life-stories of the playboy murderer, the distinguished, worldly victim, and Thaw's wife, the beautiful chorus girl and artists' model, Evelyn Nesbit, that made the case one of the most sensational in the country's history. Evelyn Nesbit, the model, is shown above; at the left, she appears as a dancer. Thaw said he shot White to protect his wife from the older man's attentions; one of his lawyers coined a phrase during the trial when he said Thaw had had a "brain-storm."

The Hall-Mills case had everything—a family of excellent social position was involved, a love affair between a clergyman and a church member was uncovered, bizarre witnesses appeared, and the mystery was never solved. On September 16, 1922, the bodies of the Rev. Edward Wheeler Hall and Mrs. James Mills, choir singer in his church, were found under a crab-apple tree near New Brunswick, New Jersey. They had been shot to death, and there was no possibility of suicide. The case died down through lack of evidence, but four years later a tabloid newspaper, in a shameless drive for circulation, claimed to have new evidence and Mrs. Hall, the widow (*right*), together with two of her brothers and a cousin, was charged with murder. They were acquitted after a sensational trial and terrible ordeal. Ruth Snyder, shown below with her mother, went to the electric chair for the killing (with the aid of her lover, a corset-salesman named Henry Judd Gray) of her husband, Albert Snyder. This sordid crime (the murder was done with a sash-weight) was built up by the press into a nine months' wonder, crowned by a sneak photograph of Mrs. Snyder's electrocution in Sing Sing on January 13, 1928, but it remained an epic only in brutality and stupidity, lacking all elements of classic tragedy.

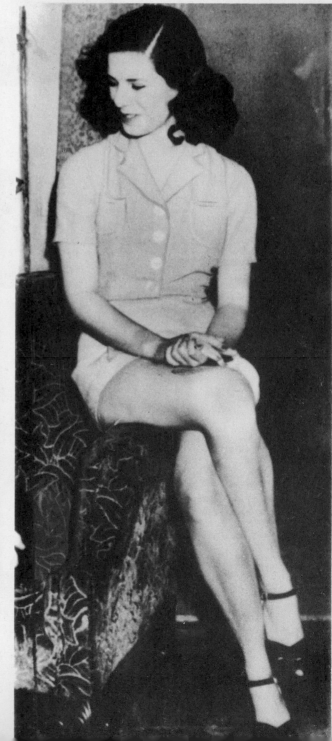

When the battered body of Mrs. Patricia Burton Lonergan (*right*) was found on October 24, 1943, in her triplex apartment in New York, the tabloid press might well have hoped for another long-term orgy, for details of the private lives of Mr. and Mrs. Lonergan offered promising material. Public interest in the case, however, was short-lived. The killer—her husband—was arrested within a very brief time, and the reading public went back to reading the war news.

IS THERE A CRIMINAL TYPE?

All the women on this page and the next, with a single exception, were accused and convicted of killing another human being. Some were accomplices, some did the fatal deed themselves. The exception was a victim of murder. Could you, without reading the captions, spot the criminals?

The friendly and competent-looking woman at the left might b on her way to a meeting of the woman's club in almost any com munity. She is actually leaving prison where she has served 1 years of her 30-year term for second degree murder. Clara Phillips known as the Los Angeles Tiger Woman, was convicted of ham mering to death Alberta Meadows, whom she suspected of "friend liness" with her husband, in 1923. One would scarcely suppos that the amiable, innocent face of th woman in the center above is that o a murderer on her way to the electri chair, but such is the case. Mrs. Iren Schroeder and her lover, Walte Glenn Dague, were convicted of kil ing a Pennsylvania State highwa patrolman in December, 1929. O February 23, 1931, Mrs. Schroede had the dubious distinction of bein the first woman to be electrocuted i Pennsylvania.

At the left is Winnie Ruth Judd i her cell in the Arizona State Priso This fragile creature on October 1 1931, shot and killed two wome friends, and shipped their dismen bered bodies in two trunks and suitcase to Los Angeles. She wa caught, convicted, and sentenced be hanged, but at a special hearin held 72 hours before the schedule execution was judged insane.

Despite her confession that she gave the girl morphine to ease her pain, there has been considerable doubt as to the guilt of Dr. Alice Lindsay Wynekoop (*above*), here shown on November 24, 1933, three days after her daughter-in-law was found dead in the doctor's operating room. Dr. Wynekoop, a highly respected Chicago physician, had served nearly fourteen years of her 25-year sentence when she was released (at the age of 76) from the State Women's Reformatory at Dwight, Illinois, on December 28, 1947, with a serious heart condition. Dr. Orlando Scott, a criminologist in private practice in Chicago, announced that in October 1948 he had administered a lie detector test to Dr. Wynekoop at her request, and that it showed she was telling the truth when she denied killing her son's wife. Madeline Webb, shown below, with her mother, is on trial with two men whose accomplice she was (although she was not present when the strangling took place) in the murder of Mrs. Susan Flora Reich, a wealthy refugee, living in New York City.

The smartly dressed woman above, getting into the car, is Helen Wills Love, on her way to the women's prison at Tehachapi, California, for the shooting of Harry Love, and the photograph below (of the only face which might be described by the amateur as untrustworthy) is that of Elizabeth Short (The Black Dahlia), murder victim.

IN BAD COMPANY

The pert and cheerful little creature above (*left*) is Celia Cooney, known as the Bobbed-hair Bandit. She is standing with her husband, Edward Sebastian Cooney, shortly after their capture in May 1924. They admitted to ten assaults and robberies which had netted them some $1600 and a sentence of from ten to twenty years in prison. (They were actually paroled in 1931.) Bonnie Parker (*above, right*), playfully pointing a gun at Clyde Barrow, did not stop at robbery. This couple and their gang were credited with twelve murders before they were themselves killed by Texas deputies in 1934.

Two of the various women in the life of the notorious John Dillinger are shown here. "The Woman in Red," as Anna Sage was known, appears at the left smiling on her way to deportation in 1936 after she had put the finger on the outlaw; Evelyn Frechette (*above*), after Dillinger's death, made capital by recounting her experiences in a carnival show entitled "Gang Busters."

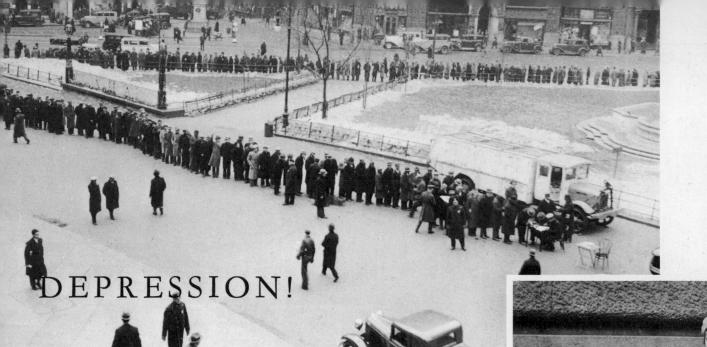

DEPRESSION!

The beginning of the nineteen-thirties saw American life gradually transformed by the onset of the Great Depression—that baffling illness of the economic system that whittled down people's incomes, robbed them of their jobs, and in millions of cases even threatened them with starvation. Here we remind you of some of the few visible signs of an almost invisible plague. Above, an endless line of men waits outside City Hall, New York, to register for snow-removal jobs; at the right, a formerly prosperous woman sells apples on the sidewalk; below, a moneyless Pittsburgh family barters eggs for groceries.

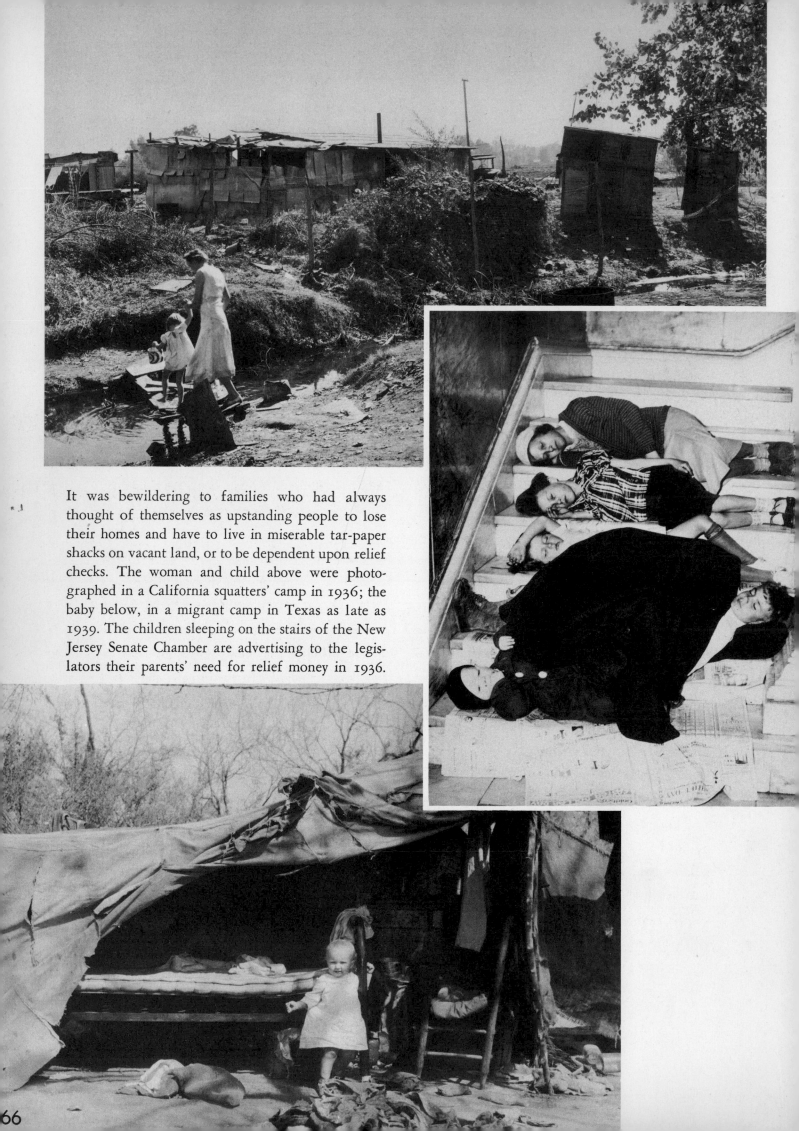

It was bewildering to families who had always thought of themselves as upstanding people to lose their homes and have to live in miserable tar-paper shacks on vacant land, or to be dependent upon relief checks. The woman and child above were photographed in a California squatters' camp in 1936; the baby below, in a migrant camp in Texas as late as 1939. The children sleeping on the stairs of the New Jersey Senate Chamber are advertising to the legislators their parents' need for relief money in 1936.

THE LETTER OF AN UNKNOWN WOMAN TO MRS. HERBERT HOOVER AND MRS. FRANKLIN D. ROOSEVELT

I AM forty-seven years old. I have spent twenty of those years, it seems to me now, looking for ways to waste time—stretching several hours of housework over a day, window shopping for an extra pair of white gloves, playing second-rate bridge, getting a novel at the library every day or two that told about people as romantic as I once thought I'd be. Jim and I have always considered that we had spent a pretty successful and happy life together. But this is 1932, and I am suddenly facing the fact that time is all I have left, and I simply don't know how to use it. Perhaps you can help me. Of course, we ourselves haven't been hit so badly. My husband has had several salary cuts and that's meant taking our younger son out of college. But, after all, his father didn't go to college and he got along pretty well. There are people, though, in this town, right on my own street, who aren't so lucky. The little girl next door, for instance. She's been married for three years and has two babies. Four months ago her husband lost his job. Several houses farther down there are old Mr. and Mrs. Thrasher, who haven't any children at all and who lost every cent when the bank failed this spring. Just across the street there are the Formans. He has been out of work for weeks, but recently she managed to get back her job as a stenographer. Still that's hardly a satisfactory arrangement with three small children to look after. The strange thing is that several years ago I wouldn't have known these neighbors of mine. Now, suddenly, I'm necessary to them and I feel important for the first time since my children were young. Two or three times a week I go next door and give that child a hand in the housework. And watch the babies so she can have a little time to herself. I haven't a maid any more, but I always did like to cook and it's no trouble to make a few extra biscuits and take them down the street to the Thrashers. Jim has fixed up a swing and a sandbox in the back yard and the children can play there all afternoon as well as not. That's the kind of thing our grandmothers did, and if we've learned to be neighbors again, perhaps this depression will have taught us something. Something—but is it enough? You see, I don't go in much for club work. I'm no good at organizing committees and that kind of thing, and, frankly, I don't care much about it. I can't say that I really understand what caused the depression or what's going to end it. But I can take the neighborhood children for a ride or sew rompers for the babies next door. It's just a beginning, of course, but is the beginning to be the end? Or is there something else that I can do? There must be thousands of women like me without much money, but with plenty of time. I am writing to you because our problems are your problems, aren't they? After all, we are the women of America. . . . . Haven't you an answer to give us?

From *McCall's Magazine*, October 1932.

The letter on the preceding page conveys a good deal of what was going on in the minds of innumerable American women during the Depression years: the blow to their pride; the discovery that what had been happening to them was not just their own secret disgrace, but something shared by others too; their neighborly efforts to help one another; and their frantic feeling that surely somebody must know the answer and be able to bring this trouble to an end. "I haven't a maid any more, but I always did like to cook," wrote the Unknown Woman; the girl pictured below symbolizes the forced occupation of the kitchen by a great many women who up to that time had thought of dinner as something you ordered and the cook prepared.

Possibly the fact that so many women saw their kitchens with fresh—and dismayed—eyes in the Depression years hastened the rebellion against the sort of inconvenience and ugliness shown in the picture at the left. It happens to be a farm kitchen, but many kitchens in towns and cities were just as awkward and no more beautiful.

A dream kitchen of the late thirties and early forties is shown at the right. Scientific planning had produced an efficient workshop, with step-saving units, electrical devices without number, fluorescent lighting, and storage space for everything. And the interior decorator had got in some good licks as well. The deep-freeze had not yet appeared as standard equipment but was on its way.

Conversation Pieces of the Thirties

Gone With the Wind was published in June 1936 and shortly thereafter a general topic of conversation was the burning question, "Did Scarlett ever get Rhett back?" A million copies were sold in six months, and Frank Luther Mott in his *Golden Multitudes* (1947) put the sale of the book at three million and said that its distribution in this country "has now surpassed that of *Uncle Tom's Cabin*, its nearest rival for the topmost position among novels in all the history of American readership." Other widely discussed books of the decade included *Live Alone and Like It*, by Marjorie Hillis; John Steinbeck's *Grapes of Wrath*; *The Good Earth*, by Pearl Buck; Hervey Allen's *Anthony Adverse*; *Life With Father*, by Clarence Day; and *The Late George Apley*, by John Marquand.

"In sheer readability, it is surpassed by nothing in American fiction."
NEW YORK TIMES

GONE WITH the WIND

by MARGARET MITCHELL

THIRTY-SIX PRINTINGS . . . 1,303,000 COPIES

A cult of the early thirties which was taken very seriously by a few practitioners and very irreverently by everybody else was nudism. James Thurber's drawing appeared in *The New Yorker*, March 11, 1933.

Live Alone AND LIKE IT

A GUIDE FOR THE EXTRA WOMAN
80th to 90th Thousand

By MARJORIE HILLIS

"See how beautifully your wife has caught the spirit of nudism, Mr. Spencer."

On December 11, 1936, in a radio speech which began, "Now at long last. . . ." King Edward VIII of England abdicated his throne to marry an American woman, the fashionable and witty Mrs. Wallis Warfield Simpson. Feeling ran high, not only throughout the British Empire, but also in the United States, and Prime Minister Baldwin, who had opposed the match because Mrs. Simpson was a divorcee, was excoriated by some, applauded by others with equal intensity. The Duke and Duchess of Windsor, as the principals of this stormy match were later known, appear in the photograph below, some twelve years later, dancing at the Greenbrier in White Sulphur Springs.

A new kind of Society was born in the thirties—Café Society. Society as it had been in the days of Mrs. Astor suffered a long slow decline after her death, and the Depression of the thirties further tarnished the former lustre of the inheritors of wealth. Moreover, some of the socially elect began to discover more entertaining company outside their own ranks, and the high-grade speakeasy and its successor, the quite legal restaurant or night club, offered a place where scions of old and wealthy families could rub (and bend) elbows with celebrities of Broadway and Hollywood. On the whole, the foundation of Café Society was publicity, and the same force made pretty Brenda Frazier, shown above at the Stork Club, known to the country as the "No. 1 Glamor Girl" among New York's débutantes of 1937.

Robert Day's cartoon at the right, which appeared in *The New Yorker* for June 3, 1933, was only one of the many references of the time to the peripatetic habits of the energetic First Lady of the land.

"For gosh sakes, here comes Mrs. Roosevelt!"

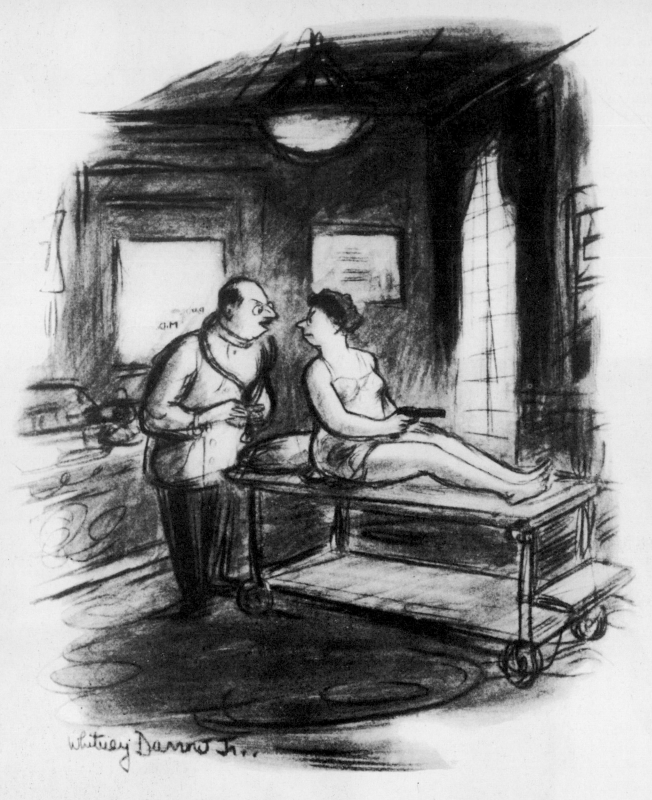

"I can't help you, Mrs. Benton, unless you give me your complete confidence."

The doctor in this cartoon by Whitney Darrow, Jr. which appeared in *The New Yorker* for March 20, 1937, appears to be intent upon a physical, rather than psychological, examination of his patient. But the far-reaching influence of psychoanalysis is clearly reflected in both doctor and patient. And indeed, a considerable number of the well-to-do women who lay down in doctors' offices did so on psychoanalysts' couches, where they were expected to give their fullest confidence—while argument raged as to the merits of this protracted treatment, and people talked glibly about neuroses and complexes, and only the simple-minded would repeat a dream at the breakfast table.

The sport of skiing won its great popularity in the thirties. At the beginning of the decade, only comparatively few people risked life and limb on snowy hillsides, but by 1937, snow trains and snow buses were operating, weather permitting, out of cities from Boston to San Francisco, and in 1948 the number of ski fans was near three million. The picture above is from Sun Valley.

The incomparable Babe Didrikson didn't ever play much football (although she did everything else) but the picture at the right, taken in 1932, demonstrates that she'd be no slouch at that either. That was the year she won the National Women's Track and Field team championship single-handed and qualified for five events in the Olympics. She was allowed to enter only three, in the course of which she broke a world's record hurdling, threw a javelin farther than any other woman had done, and tied for first place in the high jump. More recently, as Mrs. George Zaharias, she made headlines by winning the British Women's Amateur Golf Championship in the summer of 1947.

Radio's coming of age in the nineteen-thirties opened new fields for women as well as men. On this page are shown three women (they represent a large company) whose striking successes on the air have come from widely dissimilar talents. Mary Margaret Mc-Bride (*right*) was an established writer before she turned to radio, but her real reputation was made on the air waves, where her devoted listeners are numbered in the millions. Her numerous honors include a rose named for her, and November 22, 1940, was proclaimed "Mary Margaret McBride Day" by the Governor of Missouri. Gracie Allen (*lower right*), the dafter member of the popular team of Burns and Allen, has had a remarkable national following since the early nineteen-thirties.

Dorothy Thompson (*above*) is listed in *Who's Who* as a newspaper columnist, lecturer, radio commentator. During the twenties she was a foreign correspondent, and later she had the honor of being ordered to leave Germany by Hitler's express order, because of her outspoken criticism of the Nazis. In the late thirties, when the long shadow of coming German aggression was spreading over Europe, Miss Thompson, as a radio commentator, was eloquent in her efforts to rouse American public opinion.

The revolution of 1927, when talking films first appeared, turned the motion picture industry upside down. The immediate popularity of the sound track (despite a few die-hards) had made it abundantly clear that the silent film was doomed. Greta Garbo, who had resisted all attempts to force her into talking pictures on the theory that her English was not yet good enough, was persuaded to play the lead in *Anna Christie* in 1930. It was a part in which her strong Swedish accent was in character, and she won, if possible, even greater popularity than before. The photograph (*left*) shows her in this role.

In 1931 Katharine Cornell (*right*) opened in *The Barretts of Wimpole Street*, a play about the courtship of Robert Browning and the delicate Elizabeth Barrett. Since Helen Hayes gave her memorable portrayal of Queen Victoria (produced in 1935) these two actresses have shared the title of "First Lady of the American Stage," but Miss Cornell was generally given the honor prior to the production of *Victoria Regina*. However, the great rise of the motion picture, and the consequent lessening of interest in the stage in the country as a whole, had by this time brought far more glittering fame and fortune to film stars than to Broadway stars.

The Thin Man (*above*), as presented in 1934 by Myrna Loy and William Powell, was a highly refreshing novelty, in that a murder mystery was handled as a high-spirited comedy and a clearly sophisticated married couple were shown as being in love with each other. In the same year came *It Happened One Night*, the picture that won the Academy award as the outstanding production of the year. The two stars, Claudette Colbert and Clark Gable (*right*), also won the awards for the best performances. Another box-office attraction of 1934 was a very young lady, Miss Shirley Temple, here shown with Spencer Tracy in *Now I'll Tell*.

The regular movie audience of the thirties was estimated to be eighty-five million people a week, and those who wonder at the paucity of movies that reflect the grim conditions of the times (a notable exception, of course, being John Steinbeck's *The Grapes of Wrath*, produced in 1940) may ponder the sentiments of movie exhibitors in Middletown as reported by the Lynds in *Middletown in Transition* (1937): "They have wanted the movies more than ever to supply the lacks in their existence. The 'fairyland' type of picture has been more popular than ever—the type of picture that lifts people into a happy world of gaiety and evening clothes; and both our business people and working class have shied off serious and sad pictures —they have too much of that at home!"

Three types of movie stars—all of whom made their reputations in the thirties—are shown on this page. Bette Davis (*above*) became a star after her memorable performance in *Of Human Bondage* (1934). She is shown here in the part of the heroine in *Dark Victory*, a part she played with tragic intensity. Irene Dunne (*above, right*) appears with Charles Boyer in *Love Affair*. A good singing voice, a delicate air of breeding, and marked intelligence set Miss Dunne apart from a number of film stars. Katharine Hepburn appears at the right with James Stewart in a scene from *The Philadelphia Story*, a bright spot of 1940. Miss Hepburn, famous for her informal overalls, her dislike of publicity, and her disregard for the accepted rules of Hollywood procedure, nevertheless won an Oscar in 1933 for her performance in *Morning Glory*.

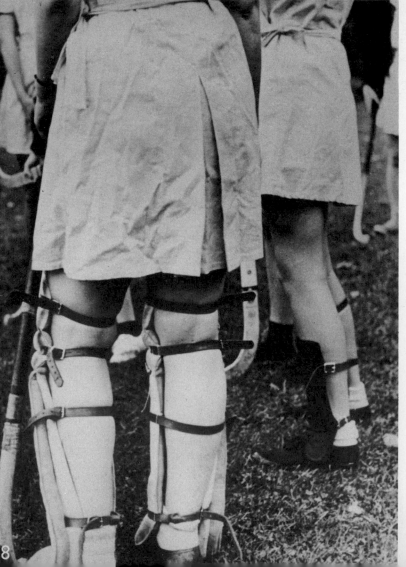

BRIGHT COLLEGE YEARS

The majority opinion on college education for women in 1871 was expressed by the Rev. Dr. John Todd when he declared, "The normal structure, the physiology, the diseases, the habit of thought and feeling of the female properly bans her from the halls of higher learning." There was, however, a courageous minority who held the opposite view. A prosperous brewer of Poughkeepsie, Matthew Vassar, was one of them. In his speech to his Board of Trustees delivered in February 1861, he said, "At different periods, I have regarded various plans [for the disposition of his fortune] with favor, but these have all been dismissed until the subject of erecting and endowing a college for the education of young women was presented. . . . The novelty, grandeur, and benignity of the idea arrested my attention. . . . It occurred to me that woman, having received from her Creator the same intellectual constitution as man, has the same right as man to intellectual culture and development." Four years later Vassar College opened.

The photograph above shows three Wellesley students in 1888. By that time Mount Holyoke, Elmira, Vassar, Wellesley, Smith, and Bryn Mawr were established institutions; Radcliffe, Barnard, the Women's College at Brown University, the College for Women at Western Reserve, and the Newcomb Memorial College at Tulane University had been opened; and, west of the Alleghenies, the policy of co-education permitted women to share the facilities of most of the state universities. This did not mean, however, that higher education for women had universal approval. Girls who went to college ran the risk of being considered peculiar, awesome, dangerously radical, or unfeminine—or all four. The co-eds on the opposite page, comfortably studying in a dormitory at the University of Minnesota in the thirties, faced none of the criticism or ridicule that must have been the lot of the Wellesley girls above.

Although the evidence is imperfect, it is fair to assume that the dimensions of college girls have changed too in the past fifty years. One would not expect to find the sturdy legs of the Vassar girls attired for hockey on the opposite page beneath the flowing skirts of the Vassar girl toying with a portiere and a rose, shown at the right.

Extra-curricular activities of the nineties are here represented. The editorial board of the Wellesley *Prelude* appear to be pondering a matter of policy; the musicians belonged to the Vassar Banjo Club; outdoor sports, of a somewhat stationary sort, are illustrated by the Vassar girl playing tennis. (A photograph of the archery club at Wells College appears earlier in this book, on page 16.) Matthew Vassar's ideas on exercise were expressed as follows: "As physical health is more or less indebted to physical resolution and vigor, I recommend progression in this department by the erection of a few simple swings on cross framework located on the lawns."

The Wellesley crews shown above and at the left were selected, one is surprised to learn, not for their ability to row, but for their voices! The duty of the crews before 1893 was not to win races, but to row quietly to a cove and then serenade the campus. By way of contrast, the 1949 crew is shown below.

The classic argument in favor of co-education is that it enables girls and men to work together and play together as naturally and sensibly as, for example, the group below, who are working busily (and unselfconsciously) on the student newspaper, the Minnesota *Daily*. It is true that before the nineteen-twenties, the presence of men on the campuses of the women's colleges was so rare as to be an almost painful novelty—certainly painful for the man. Even during prom weekends, there was so little provision for entertaining one's partner, so many rules, so many chaperones, that the season was scarcely an hilarious one. The couple on the right—in 1905—had little choice but a stroll around the Vassar campus the day after a prom. (The prom, by the way, had begun in broad daylight so that the girls could be in bed by midnight.) Had it been midwinter, visitors might have been treated to an exhilarating game of ice hockey, as above.

Before the advent of Martha Graham as a serious influence the dance as practiced in most women's colleges (outside of social dancing, of course) was generally of two kinds. Both are represented here in the upper and middle pictures, taken in the mid-twenties at Wells.

Quite clearly, the students above are performing a folk dance of some kind, and one likes to think that natural high spirits rather than inattention, account for their lack of precision. The meaning of the dance at the left is not so clear. It could symbolize general satisfaction or overcoming barriers in the path of life—or have you by any chance another suggestion?

Twenty years later, college girls were more sophisticated. The group of Vassar girls at the right are almost certainly well acquainted with the music of Roy Harris, Aaron Copland, and Charles Ives, as well as the fine points of New Orleans and Chicago jazz. On their walls hang reproductions of pictures by Braque, Rouault, Chagall, and Ben Shahn. They discuss the latest articles in *The Partisan Review* and books published by the New Directions Press.

The photograph above was taken in 1939, but, except for the length of the student's skirt, it might have been taken any time in the following decade. Marion Bacon, in her book *Life at Vassar*, published in 1940, said, "Bare legs and socks, winter and summer, have been standard for the thirties; sweaters and skirts the accepted campus costume for the past twenty years." The serious looking girls below were photographed in a class in political science (at Vassar) and give a fair sample of the appearance and interests of contemporary undergraduate life.

Sun bathing hit the colleges, as well as the rest of the country, in the thirties. Letters, as an invaluable link with the outside world, continue, even in an age of freedom, to be important in college life. It seems unlikely that the girl crouched on the ground is as impatient as all that to read a letter from home. (See page 188.)

There is little of the cloister in the scene below taken on the Vassar campus shortly before World War II swept the grounds of women's colleges bare of male visitors. The trend in social regulations in most women's colleges during the past few decades had been to reduce the number of rules and to depend more and more on the students' own sense of personal responsibility, with the emphasis shifting gradually over the years from strict propriety to decent behavior.

It is not surprising to find that women coming out of college in the years from 1890 to 1915 so often threw themselves into militant social reform. It was the period of the crusader. The next period, lasting through the twenties, reflected the general upsurge of prosperity and the graduates were more likely to turn to the new fields of business where salaries were certainly higher. Three reasons for this shift seem plausible: 1) the crusaders had done such a good job that social injustice had actually lessened with improved working conditions; 2) it was no longer a bold and courageous thing to go to college and the student bodies had therefore fewer girls of the adventurous, social-minded pioneer type; 3) with the winning of universal suffrage, the earlier objectives had been won, and the entrance of women into the executive levels of the world of business was the last assertion of equal rights with men.

And what have we here? Both of these photographs were taken at Vassar in the mid-forties. A temporary aftermath of World War II was the admission of groups of veterans to various of the women's colleges when the men's colleges and universities were unable to handle the vast numbers of men entitled to college training under the G.I. Bill of Rights. Some of Vassar's men students appear at the left. But the scene above is no temporary phenomenon. This is a song session in the course of the Vassar Summer Institute for Family and Community Living that has been going on vigorously since 1926.

The drawings on this page and the next appeared in two books by Anne Cleveland and Jean Anderson—*Vassar, A Second Glance* (published in 1942) and *Everything Correlates* (published in 1946). They scarcely require explanation.

"The first letter I've had for *three* days and it's from my mother!"

". . . and how can we ever expect to have international accord when we don't even have an editorial policy toward Russia?"

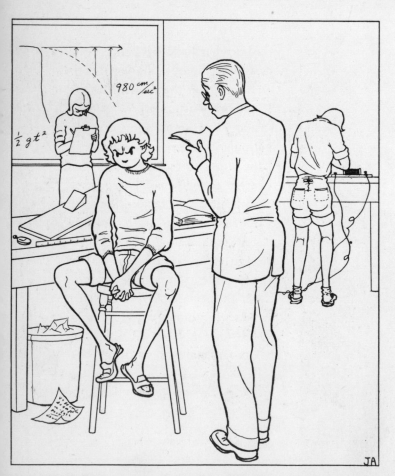

"But Miss Witherspoon, just what *is* there about the law of gravity that you find yourself unable to accept?"

"No, Bill — with your low frustration tolerance and my aggression patterns, it would never work."

"I thought you said he had the most interesting mind you ever met!"

"And so we're making this survey to find out how a representative section of the community feels about a government policy of deficit spending."

When we consider the integral relationships unquestionably inherent in such a frame of reference, it becomes apparent that certain basic characteristics, hitherto attributed by scholars to external influences, or assumed to have been superimposed at a later date, must, of necessity . . .

"I must show you the room I had when I was in college."

JOBS FOR THE COMELY

Above are two burlesque queens of the early years of the century, Frances Thropp and Lydia Thompson. Below, a bevy of burlesque queens are picknicking with managers' wives, and presenting an aspect somewhat more hearty than sexy.

he market value of feminine comeliness has always been high, but he nature of the market changes from generation to generation as the standards of propriety and desirability change. In the early years of he century a woman could put her beauty on the marriage market, but he could hardly exhibit herself publicly for pay without losing her eputation, especially if the exhibition could be classified as exposure. lthough the ladies of the burlesque on the opposite page may have een models of discreet behavior, they were sternly frowned on by ost of their contemporaries. But a change was coming, and the miracle as wrought, not by young radicals defying a puritanic tradition, but y hard-headed business. The Atlantic City Bathing Beauty Contest, auagurated in 1921, was set for the Wednesday following Labor Day, e time most summer visitors departed. The purpose of the contest, cording to the book of rules, was "to develop a higher appreciation the beautiful in young womanhood by the American public." And e eligibility rules were careful to ban those traditionally considered abious characters; not only "actresses and artist's models" but also vidows and divorcees." The contest proved to be a smashing financial ccess. Charles Merz in *The Great American Bandwagon* (1928) rote, "One hundred thousand visitors is the average estimate of the umber of people who remain for the four days of the carnival, and at e low estimate of ten dollars spent per day per person this means four illion dollars." The photograph above shows the Bathing Beauties of 23; Miss America of 1940 appears at the right.

How far things had gone by 1940 or thereabouts is suggested by these two photographs of Rose Louise Hovick, better known as Gypsy Rose Lee, strip-teaser extraordinary. Miss Lee, after entrancing audiences in the *Streets of Paris* show at the New York World's Fair, turned to more intellectual pastimes. She was the author of a best-selling detective story, *The G-String Murders,* in 1941, and thereafter contributed to various magazines, including *Harper's Bazaar, The New Yorker,* the *American Mercury,* and *Collier's.* She also exhibited her paintings at the Guggenheim Galleries in New York.

A leading principle of the art of profitable exposure is, "One thing at a time." We present two pictures of this artist because her celebrated legs are invisible in the photograph at the right. Readers may—or may not —be surprised to know that Miss Lee was the war-sweetheart of 18 regiments.

The cheerful girl demonstrating the coffee-vending machine is not a strip-teaser; far from it. She simply illustrates a further development in the nature of the market for comeliness, another step in the progress of beauty for business' sake, so profitably begun in Atlantic City. She is engaged in what had become by the thirties an accepted practice—commercial exposure. It had been discovered that legs helped sales (as they enlivened parades—see the drum-majorette on page 116) no matter what the product so advertised was. Happily for American business, thighs, though still interesting, had become respectable, as a glance at even the most select bathing beach in the nineteen-forties plainly demonstrated.

Another noted strip-teaser, Ann Corio (*above*), who has said of her early years, "I wanted to dance, but I studied piano at a convent for two years," was working as a showgirl in Earl Carroll's *Sketch Book* when the profitable idea of strip-tease occurred to her. Within a year she had progressed from $35 to $300 a week. "I had to earn my living in some way and disrobing seemed the most artistic way to earn it," she has testified, adding that when her act was a big success, she was delighted because "it meant that the beautiful thoughts I had in mind while performing had caught on."

In the nineteen-thirties American business made a big discovery: tha personable young women were great asset in jobs which involve meeting the public. And the youn women made a corresponding dis covery: that such jobs were worth getting. United Airlines began em ploying flight stewardesses on Ma 15, 1930, and although the airme at first resented their presence, befor long all the other airlines had fo lowed suit. Until World War all stewardesses had to be registere nurses, and press agents called them the "Florence Nightingales of th Airways." At the left are some Ame ican Airlines stewardesses of the earl nineteen-thirties.

Air stewardesses should be attractive, well-groomed, courteous, diplomatic, healthy, unmarried, from 21 to 28 years in age, from 5 feet to 5 feet 6 inches tall, and not over 130 pounds in weight. No wonder they have a way of leaving the service to get married. Below, a United Airlines stewardess checks in a passenger.

A flight stewardess at her station in the rear of a DC-4 demonstrates, with the smile demanded by public relations men and now automatically assumed by almost everybody in the presence of a camera, how she can telephone to the pilot.

Arthur Murray, the man who built dance-teaching into a big business, grew up on New York's East Side, did his first dance-teaching at Castle House, the school set up by Irene and Vernon Castle during the great dance-boom of the years 1912-17, and after teaching the fox-trot by correspondence for a time, from Atlanta, moved to New York and in the mid-twenties set up the school which he has maintained ever since. He has been so careful to select as instructors girls with agreeable manners and impeccable deportment that dance-instruction has become an occupation sought after even by many college graduates who might have been expected to choose a calling that made more intellectual demands. It is, moreover, of possible social significance that the girl of good family and established position who becomes a dance instructor does not lose caste thereby as she most certainly would have in an earlier day—unless she was teaching children.

At the right is Arthur Murray himself; below are two demonstrations of correct dancing by his instructors.

Every year nearly 4,000 girls come to New York in the hope of succeeding in the most glamorous of all jobs—that of model. The ten per cent who have the right combination of figure, photogenic features, poise, and persistence are absorbed into the well-organized fifteen-million-dollar-a-year industry that the modeling business has become. Three Powers models appear on this page.

The three pictures on this page reveal the versatility of Ellen Brooks, a Powers model. On the opposite page, Peggy O'Connor poses at the top, Jackie Burns at the right, and Helen Bennett below. Twenty-five dollars an hour is not unusual pay, and top flight models get as much as forty, but their bills run high for make-up, care of their hair, and clothes, especially shoes.

Girls with the "natural" look have superseded the gorgeous, exotic beauties of a few years back, although the high style girls are still more sleek and sophisticated than the outdoor type or the junior. The fourth general class is the special model, who has outstandingly good hands, feet, legs, or head. Fashion models must be 5' 6" to 5' 10" (with heels) and wear a size 12 or 14. The model has to draw a fine line between going to enough parties to be seen regularly at fashionable gatherings, and getting enough sleep to appear always fresh and clear-eyed for work. Possibly ten per cent of the models in New York have been débutantes as this is another occupation which has become socially acceptable.

A corner of Elizabeth Arden's New York establishment is shown above, a demonstration of her exercises appears below, and the business wizard herself is at the right. Born Florence Nightingale Graham, Miss Arden arrived in New York (from Toronto) in 1908, and by 1915 had a flourishing business of her own. In 1929 she refused an offer of $15,000,000 for her world-famous beauty business, and despite the Depression, she opened seven new salons and four department store outlets between 1929 and 1935. Her racing stable is equally successful; in 1945 she was at the top of the list of money-earning owners and her Jet Pilot won the Kentucky Derby in 1947.

Closest rival to Elizabeth Arden in the field where American women spend in the neighborhood of seven hundred million dollars a year is Helena Rubinstein (*right*). When she opened her beauty salon in New York in 1914 she already had establishments in London and Paris, and her business has expanded more or less consistently ever since. The young lady below demonstrating what is called in the mystical language of the beauty world "the Electro-Tonic treatment" is not a regular operator but a member of the Fokine School of Ballet, part of an elaborate show marking the opening of a new salon.

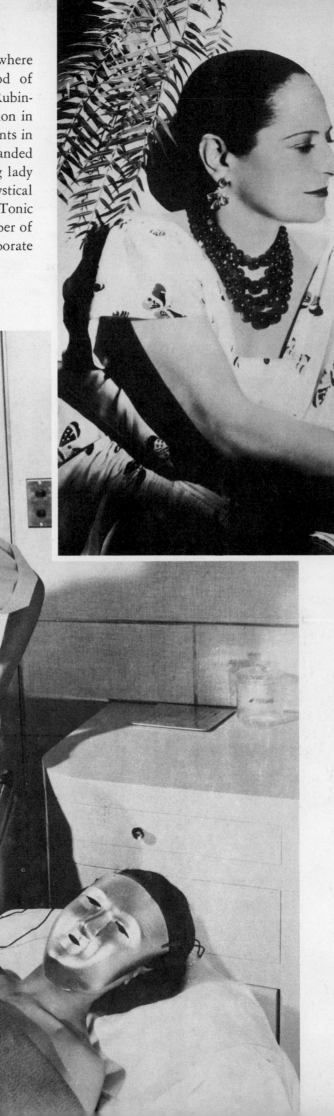

At the left Ann Delafield subjects a new pupil at the DuBarry Success School to a "candid scrutiny" before prescribing the treatment that will enable her "to see the possibilities in *her* future; how to grasp life . . . and beauty . . . in her hands; how to be the alert, vital, charming person she *can* be if she understands the fundamentals of physical fitness and good grooming." In the rigorous six-weeks course at this school where the student works three hours a day, five days a week, at the serious business of self-improvement, she is given instruction in make-up, hair styling (as shown below), posture, walking, dancing, and voice production, while her excess poundage is being reduced. There are boarding schools as well as day schools for beauty where the woman of determination (and ample means) can really concentrate on this beauty business. Elizabeth Arden operates two—one in Maine in the summer, one in Arizona in the winter—where iron discipline is maintained in the midst of luxury.

And Now—

Any chronicle of change must take account of those influences and interests that go right on from generation to generation, altering only in detail. Before we begin to examine the evidences of new directions that seem most striking in the nineteen-forties, let us look at some of the older preoccupations that remain. First, the church, in whose service women continue to play usually humble but indispensable parts—teaching in the Sunday School, contributing the floral decorations, or, as below, preparing for a church supper. The building at the left stands near Franconia, New Hampshire; the ladies of St. Thomas's Church, below, are Kentuckians; and the bottom photograph shows a Sunday School picnic in a West Virginia mining town. All represent a force that has changed but little in its impact on American women.

As a place for social gatherings, however, the church has become less important for the more prosperous, as the Lynds point out in *Middletown in Transition*: "One has only to compare the way a working-class population leaves its church services . . . lingering to talk in the aisles and on the steps, and the brisk dignity with which the business class leave their Presbyterian Church . . . to sense some of this differential need for places and occasions of social meeting."

Another perennial influence is the women's club. Hardly a community in the country exists in which at least one group of women does not gather regularly for study or unalloyed pleasure, and national associations devoted to women's interests are almost numberless.

And another perennial activity, both delicious and exhausting, is shopping—an occupation which daily engages hours of the time of millions of women. At the left is Kenneth Hayes Miller's painting, "The Fitting Room"; below, a photograph with a Texas flavor, taken at the Nieman-Marcus store in Dallas. Foreigners on arriving in the United States are invariably amazed to see to what a degree American women handle the family finances; even some Americans may be surprised to know that in this country women own seventy per cent of the private wealth.

Endlessly continuing, also, is criticism by adults of the distressing customs and manners of the younger generation. Early in this century the adolescent girl of the family was likely to arouse dismay by her tomboy behavior. In the nineteen-twenties she was called down for smoking and staying out late with the boys. In more recent years, she has disturbed her elders by—among other things—her orgies of juvenile sentiment. Above, a crowd of bobby-soxers besiege Van Johnson; at the right, a fifteen-year-old admirer of Frank Sinatra makes no secret of her adoration of "The Voice"; and below, some teen-agers demonstrate satisfaction with Sinatra's singing at the Paramount Theatre, New York.

Always, too, there is the problem of the older woman: how can she maintain her dignity as a person after the chief domestic tasks of her life have been completed? As time goes on, the elderly increase in relative numbers; smaller houses and apartments in many cases offer no room for them without perpetual frictions; and despite social security, pensions, and savings they are still likely to feel dependent, unwanted, and useless. Students of the American social scene never tire of pointing out our general accent on youth, and certainly a survey of American advertising reveals a noticeable lack of enthusiasm for the older woman. (Except around Mother's Day, when the dear old soul is suddenly remembered and her children are urged to shower her with woolen scarves and comfortable slippers.)

Some members of the durable sex (like the farm woman above at the left) demonstrate that age can mark a face with wisdom and serenity; and some (like the airplane factory worker above) are able to continue useful work that brings them pride. (In fact, the number of working women 45 years old or over increased from 2¾ million in 1940 to more than 4 million in 1947.) And now and then one comes upon a particularly vigorous specimen—like the grandmother on the bowling alley, who scores in the vicinity of 156—delighting in strenuous physical activity which would have seemed wholly incredible to her own grandmother.

As job-holder, salary-earner, wage-earner, woman has definitely arrived. In 1900, there were only a little over 5 million "gainfully employed" women in the United States (of whom about one in seven was married); by 1946 the number had swelled to over 16 million (of whom something like a third were married). Not only is it virtually taken for granted today that even the daughter of the rich, on graduating from college, will take a job—until she marries; but also, although in general women still draw smaller wages than men, and there still remain some slave-driving businesses, nevertheless legislation and union pressure and the force of changing custom have combined to bring them shorter hours, higher pay, and vastly improved conditions of work. Who at the beginning of the century would have expected a union to provide an art class like the one conducted by the International Ladies Garment Workers Union, pictured at the right? Or who would have looked forward to the maintenance by a company management of a lunch room as agreeable as the Bell System cafeteria shown below? There remains, however, a question: do as many girls today regard their jobs as careers-in-the-making, or dream of setting the world on fire, as in, say, the expanding nineteen-twenties? Or have a widespread Depression-born desire for security, and a shrinking from responsibility, made even girls with superior endowments and education content, for the most part, with secondary positions in enterprises carried and directed by men? A generalized answer is not easy; but certainly the early ardent feminists would have been surprised at the un-ardent occupation, today, of the ground they so hopefully battled for and won.

FROM PERFORMER TO SPECTATOR

That there has been a shift in the role of the American woman from that of performer to that of spectator in certain fields is perhaps a brash generalization; but the changing attitudes suggested by Robert Osborn on these two pages seem to strike a familiar note. Isn't it true that . . .

Women used to play and sing

Now they turn on the radio or phonograph

They used to paint

Now they look at pictures

They used to swim

Now they lie on the edge of the pool

They used to dance

Now they listen to the band

One of the most striking changes in American life has been the extent to which the gap between the ways of living of the rich and poor has been narrowed. One sign of this change is the servantless house—that is, the house that is built for living without servants. This picture shows the combination living and dining room in the modern house designed by Carl Koch for L.V.B. Nichols. Notice the dining table which slides through an opening in the wall into the kitchen to facilitate setting.

The enormous increase in servantless households among even the well-to-do has brought with it many new things: a wide increase in buffet entertaining, the domestication of many young husbands, who share in cooking and other household chores as their counterparts of a generation ago did not dream of doing; and a tendency toward short-order meals at casual hours except where the presence of children dictates a strict routine. Another change has to do with the making of clothes at home. During the nineteen-twenties the old-fashioned seamstress (referred to on page 52) practically disappeared as women of all income groups bought their clothes in the shops, ready-made. But the Depression brought a wave of home-dressmaking; World War II brought another one; and since then high prices have kept many a woman at her sewing-machine, like the girl pictured at the right. The estimates are that 28 million women are using the 24 million sewing machines in American homes, and that 25 per cent of all women's and children's clothes are now made at home. (One pattern company sold 100 million patterns in 1947.)

"Do you happen to know where we could find a good sitter?"

Whitney Darrow Jr.'s drawing at the left appeared in *The New Yorker* of June 9, 1945. It is improbable that any reader of the magazine missed the point; it is also improbable that the picture would have been published twenty years earlier. For although it has long been the custom for a servantless family to hire a high-school girl or college student, or unattached older woman, to stay in the house with the children while the parents went out of an evening, baby-sitting did not become big business until the nineteen-forties. An article in the November 20, 1948, issue of the *Saturday Evening Post* calls it "a craft dominated by a militant minority of 2 million high school girls extracting at least $750 million a year," and states that although half the American population over 12 is engaged in it regularly or sporadically, the supply falls short of the demand. The high success of the movie *Sitting Pretty*, in which Clifton Webb took the part of an unorthodox baby-sitter, reflected the fact that the quest for an adequate and responsible understudy has become the preoccupation of millions of Americans.

If the gods and goddesses of a people are to be loved as well as worshipped, they must be thought of as sharing the life of the people. Hence the elaborate pains taken by Hollywood to photograph Joan Crawford hanging the wash on the line and mopping the floor, and Ann Sheridan busily at work on a salad.

We like our stars to be glamorous on the screen but home girls at heart. So here is Joan Fontaine merrily merrily gardening (*below*). She is also reported to be one of the best cooks in Hollywood and you see her at the left giving her mother a taste of a new dish she is concocting. "Close pals, Joan and her mother spend considerable time in the kitchen just as they used to when Joan was a youngster," says the original caption of this picture, striking the correct domestic note.

Sometimes it takes quite an organization to portray for the rest of us the pretty naturalness of America's goddesses. Here is Deanna Durbin (*below*) with the staff and equipment necessitated by the assignment of some still pictures of her enjoying an afternoon on a yacht (which doesn't show in this picture). Traveling in a limousine, bus, and panel truck, the people involved are (from left to right): photographer, star, fashion editor, publicist, grip, hair stylist, wardrobe mistress, driver, make-up artist, electrician, driver, body make-up artist, driver.

THE GOOD LIFE: AMERICAN PLAN

It has sometimes been predicted by sociologists that in time the middle class would be ground between the upper and nether millstones of society—between the tycoons (or managerial class) and the proletariat. What, by contrast, has actually happened in the United States, as the ways of living of rich and poor have gradually converged, has been an approach, by Americans rich and poor, toward the sort of life idealized in these paintings of "Home Life in America," presented in a series of advertisements in 1946-48 by the United States Brewers Foundation. This life might be described as middle class, prosperous, comfortable, and equipped both with gadgets and with good will.

In "Family Musicale," by Mead Schaeffer (opposite page, upper picture), note that along with rustic characters appear young men in impeccable sports attire; the boy with the cello might well be a leader of his college class. In "Saturday Football Over the Radio," by Stevan Dohanos (opposite page, lower picture), you will see that mother (is this by any chance Mom?) does not care about football any more. Her job is the solid refreshments. But in "Baseball on Television," by Glenn Grohe, above, at least one girl is a baseball fan. (Of course, she may get over it when she's Mom's age.) The television set is the most expensive item in the well equipped room.

You may be assured that the family represented in the picture below—"Thanksgiving," by John Gannam—have a fine car (probably two), an electric washing machine, a deep-freeze unit; and that the well dressed daughter of the house, who is bringing out the turkey, will graduate from college and take a job as a stenographer—or, perhaps, model—until, and even after, she marries somebody like the cellist on the opposite page.

One characteristic of the women of America since the onset of the Depression has been an increased social consciousness—a growing sense of identification with the rest of society. For instance, the daughters of the fortunate are less likely to be indifferent to the fate of their less fortunate fellow-citizens, or to adopt a Lady Bountiful attitude. The new spirit often manifests itself in youth—as suggested by Anne Cleveland's cartoon at the left—but it is likely to continue, seriously, into maturity.

"How can I explain the position of organized labor to
Father when you keep passing me chocolate sauce?"

It is a sign of our times that glamor is now generally advertised as attainable by all American women, and as very easy to come by—you buy it in a jar. Few manufacturers feel today that to sell their products they must make women identify themselves mentally with the wealthy or socially elect. The snob appeal has become less potent than the appeal of glamor arrived at through purchase of the right products and through careful schooling in their appropriate use. Anybody can have it, whatever her background, for a little money and some effort. Glamor has been democratized.

So here we have the young woman of the mid-twentieth century, symbolized by this girl standing beside her private plane at a Texas ranch. She has been freed from Victorian restrictions of propriety, from the cumbersome costumes of an earlier day, from ancient prejudices about women in jobs, from the restraints of former class distinctions. She has almost certainly had a better education than her grandmother had; she can master many more gadgets (such as this plane); she probably has a better knowledge of the ways of the world, and a better-informed desire to help improve them. But she is as bewildered as any woman ever was over her choices among the demands made upon her by present-day society—those demands suggested in the Osborn cartoon at the beginning of this book. Shall she just take a job, or pursue a career? Or prepare to concentrate in the future upon being a satisfactory wife and mother? Shall she develop her cultural interests? Shall she take a leading part in the life of the community? Or shall she, like many a woman, try frantically to do all these things at once—and remain glamorous withal? A babel of conflicting counsel rings in her ears. Here she is, apparently quite ready to climb into her plane and fly anywhere. But toward what airport?

SOURCES AND ACKNOWLEDGMENTS

The sources of the pictures in this book are here listed alphabetically, and I am grateful for the kindly cooperation of each and all of them:

Air Force Photo: page 86 (WAAC guiding aircraft)

B. Altman & Co.: drawings on pages 95 (lower left), 96 (upper and lower right), 99 (center and lower left)

American Airlines: page 194 (upper)

American Museum of Natural History: page 141 (Mrs. Akeley and Mrs. Bradley)

American Tobacco Company: page 154 (Lucky Strike advertisement)

American Red Cross: page 88 (photo by Ollie Atkins upper left)

Architectural Forum: page 208 (photo by Ezra Stoller, Pictorial Services)

Elizabeth Arden: page 198, page 214 (photograph of girl)

Art Institute of Chicago: page 16 ("Croquet" by Winslow Homer)

Atlantic City Press Bureau: page 191 (Miss America)

H. A. Atwell Studio: page 137 (Millman), 142 (Stark)

Bellevue Hospital: pages 41 and 42

Bobbs, Merrill Company: page 170 (Book jacket of *Live Alone and Like It* and photograph of Marjorie Hillis)

Brookfield Zoo, Chicago: page 141 (Wide World photo of Mrs. Harkness)

Brown Brothers: page 6, 20, 21, 22 (Tuxedo), 28, 31, 34, 35, 36 (Mrs. Gilman), 38, 40 (photographs of Ella Wheeler Wilcox), 50, 54 (lower left), 56 (Nelly Bly), 58 (two upper photographs), 59 (upper), 60, 61, 62, 63, 68, 69 (two upper photographs), 71 (child labor), 116 (upper left), 117 (fortune teller and spirit photograph), 131 (Glenna Collett), 134, 135 (Annie Peck), 136 (Taylor), 151 (Mrs. Post), 155, 160, 191 (bathing beauties)

Columbia Broadcasting System: page 106 (modern television)

Children's Bureau: page 71 (Abbott and Lenroot)

Official Coast Guard Photograph: page 87 (SPAR officers)

Collier's: page 112 (photo by Jerry Cook)

Creative Art Studio: page 127 (Vassar Nursery School)

Culver Service: page 7, 23 (lower), 24, 25 (lower), 26, 29, 37 (lower), 46 (Miller Sisters), 47 (Farrar and Farrar and Telegen), 53, 57, 66 (two photographs of Mrs. Harriman), 69 (Jane Addams), 74, 75, 76, 78, 102, 145 (photograph), 148, 149 (Tango and Maxixe), 152, 190 (Thropp and Thompson), 192, 193

Dodd, Mead and Company: page 125 (page from *Elsie Dinsmore*)

Doubleday and Company: page 108 (Glasgow), 109 (George Platt Lynes photo of Edna Ferber)

Du Barry Success School: page 200

Eastern Air Lines: page 194 (right)

Eastman Kodak Company: page 23 (upper), 48 (upper), 49 (lower)

Georgia Engelhard: page 135 (photograph by Cromwell)

Everything Correlates, by Anne Cleveland and Jean Anderson: page 188, 189, and drawing on page 214

Lent by Marnie Fahr: page 15

Franklin Simon: page 144 (drawing from catalogue)

General Electric Company: page 168, 169 (new kitchen)

Grace Line: page 72 (lower left)

Greenbrier News Bureau: page 73 (lower photographs), 171 (Duke and Duchess of Windsor)

George A. Hamid Co.: page 136 (Kyle), 137 (Beehees)

Harper & Brothers: page 39 (Margaret Deland), 109 (E. St. Vincent Millay)

Harper's Weekly: page 17 (lower), 27, 77 (Gray Gables), 146, 147 (Tittle drawing), 155 (advertisement for cocktail)

Harvard University, Widener Library: page 43, 47 (Eames and Garden), 107, 154 (*Sapho*), 175 (Cornell)

Fred Harvey: page 56 (lower)

William E. Hill Collection: page 44, 45, 46 (lower), 190 (picnic)

Houghton Mifflin Company: page 108 (Willa Cather), 109 (Amy Lowell), 174 (Dorothy Thompson)

Isabella Stewart Gardner Museum: page 110 (Mrs. Gardner)

John Day Company: page 108 (Pearl Buck, photo by Glidden)

L. H. Jorud Collection: page 55 (Calamity Jane and Mrs. Collins)

International Ladies Garment Workers Union: page 205 (art class, photo by Harry Rubenstein)

League of Women Voters: page 64 (Voting machine, photo by International Film Service)

Liberty: page 156 (John Held, Jr., drawing)

Library of Congress: page 71 (lower, F.S.A. photo), 88 (lower, OWI photo by Liberman, and OWI photo of welder), 89 (OWI photo by Rittase), 90 (photos by Jack Delano), 91 (lower, OWI photo by Marjory Collins), 128 (FSA photos by Russell Lee), 166 (Hooverville, FSA photo by Dorothea Lange and baby in tent, FSA photo by Russell Lee), 201 (photos by Marion Post Wolcott), 204 (war worker)

Life: drawings by Charles Dana Gibson on pages 12, 22, 64, and by John Held, Jr. on pages 94, 150, 151

Life at Vassar, by Marion Bacon: page 178 (hockey legs), 179 (girl at curtin), 180 (tennis), 182 (girl and man), 184 (girl reading magazine), 185 (sun bathing)

J. B. Lippincott Company: page 40 (Elinor Glyn)

Little, Brown & Company: page 39 (Johnston and Farmer)

Longmans, Green Company: page 125 (illustration from *The Red Fairy Book,* edited by Andrew Lang)

Metro-Goldwyn-Mayer: page 177 (Katharine Hepburn)

Macmillan Company: page 170 (Book jacket of *Gone With the Wind* and photograph of Margaret Mitchell)

McCall's: page 92 (upper right and lower left), 96 (upper left), 98 (lower right), 167

Metropolitan Museum of Art: page 2, 13, 14, 25 (costume), 110 (class, photo by von Schnarendorf), 145 ("The Dust Storm," by John Sloan), 157, 202 ("The Fitting Room," by Kenneth Hayes Miller)

Metropolitan Picture Service: page 210 (Ann Sheridan)

Arthur Murray Studios: page 195

Museum of Modern Art, Film Library: page 11, 101, 103, 104, 105 (Clara Bow, and Joan Crawford in *Dancing Daughters*), 175 (Garbo), 176

Museum of the City of New York: page 10 (photographs by Mora), 11 (the Byron Collection), 32 and 33 (the Jacob A. Riis Collection), 70 (the Jacob A. Riis Collection), 73 (upper), 79 (center photo, from the Byron Collection)

National Broadcasting Company: page 106 (upper left), 174 (Burns and Allen)

National Archives: page 67 (Alice Roosevelt), 82 (photographs), 83 (3 upper pictures), 84, 113 (A. Adams)

New York Historical Society: page 8 (lower, photo by Rockwood), 10 (photo by Pach), 79 (top), 143 (Central Park)

New York Public Library: page 114 (librarian and child, photo by von Schnarendorf), 119

New York Telephone Company: page 51, 205 (cafeteria)

The New Yorker: page 129 (two drawings by Carl Rose), 156 (drawing by Rea Irvin), 158, 170 (drawing by James Thurber), 171 (drawing by Robert Day), 172 (drawing by Whitney Darrow, Jr.), 209 (drawing by Whitney Darrow, Jr.)

Newark Museum: page 114 (lower, photo by von Schnarendorf)

Nieman-Marcus: page 202 (photograph)

Oklahoma Historical Society: page 55 (bottom)

Robert Osborn: drawings on page 1, 206, and 207

Packard Motor Car Company: page 48 (lower)

Palm Springs Chamber of Commerce: page 81 (upper)

Philadelphia Museum of Art: page 17 ("Fairman Rogers Four-in-Hand," by Thomas Eakins)

Photo Associates: page 196 (photographing model)

John Robert Powers: page 196, 197

Public Roads Administration: page 72 (lower right)

Ethel Purtle; page 142 (photo by Chinn of Mrs. Purtle)

Queen of Fashion: page 4, 5, 92 (upper left), 122 (drawings)

RKO: page 176 (Bette Davis), 177 (Irene Dunne)

Remington Rand Company: page 49 (drawing)

Rosalind Richards' Collection: page 39 (Julia Ward Howe and Laura E. Richards)

Rinehart & Company: page 108 (painting of M. R. Rinehart by John LaValle)

Helena Rubinstein: page 199

John S. Rudd Collection: page 3 (upper left), 43 (Modjeska), 77 (upper left), 122 (photograph), 123 (upper left and lower right), 124 (boy), 125 (schoolroom), 144 (photograph), 152 (dance card)

Charles Scribner's Sons: page 39 (Edith Wharton)

Oscar Serlin: page 52 (photo by Vandamm)

Singer Sewing Machine Company: page 209 (photograph)

W. T. Smedley (From his book, *Life and Character*): page 3 (drawing), 18, 82 (drawing)

Stork Club: page 171 (Brenda Frazier)

Sun Valley: page 80 (upper photo by Toni Frissell), 173 (skier)

Theatre Guild: page 54 (lower right, photo by Vandamm)

United Air Lines: page 194 (lower left)

United States Brewers Foundation: page 212, 213

United States Department of Agriculture: page 91 (upper, photo by Forsythe), 120 (photo by Forsythe), 121 (photo by Hunton), 204 (farm woman, photo by Forsythe)

United States Marine Corps, Official Photo: page 86 (lower)

Official United States Navy Photographs: page 83 (lower), 85, 87 (upper)

Universal-International: page 211

University of Minnesota: page 178 (dormitory), 182 (newspaper)

Vassar, A Second Glance, by Anne Cleveland and Jean Anderson: page 188, 189

Vassar College, Bureau of Publications: page 71 (upper right), 113 (Josephine Roche), 115, 127 (child painting), 153, 187

Vassar College Library: page 180 (banjo club), 182 (ice hockey), 183 (modern dance), 184 (classroom), 186

Viking Press: page 109 (photo of Dorothy Parker by George Platt Lynes)

Vogue (Courtesy the Condé Nast Publications, Inc.): page 92 (lower right), 93 (two upper), 94 (lower right and photograph by Blumenfeld), 95 (upper right), 97, 98 (left), 147 (lower)

WEAF: page 174 (M. M. McBride)

Warner Brothers: page 105 (Joan Crawford), 210 (two pictures of Joan Crawford)

Wellesley College: page 179 (upper), 180 (*Prelude*), 181

Wells College: page 16 (lower), 183 (upper pictures), 185 (post office)

A. B. Wenzell (from his book, *The Passing Show*): page 18, 72 (upper)

Westinghouse: page 106 (center left and 2 right), 169 (old kitchen)
Wide World Photos: page 8 (upper), 46 (upper left), 54 (upper left), 58 (lower), 59 (upper), 65 (lower, left), 66 (upper right and bottom), 67 (two upper), 77 (bottom), 79 (bottom), 111, 113 (Dr. Sabin), 116 (Guinan on desk), 117 (Margery), 118, 130, 131 (two Ederle pictures), 132, 133, 137 (Cody), 139, 140, 149 (Goodman), 155 (Carrie Nation and boy), 159, 161, 162, 163, 164, 165, 166 (asleep on stairs), 173 (Didrikson), 203, 204 (bowling)
William P. Wolfe Organization: page 80 (lower), 81 (lower), 215
Women's Bureau, Department of Labor: page 36 (center)
Yale University Art Gallery: page 37 ("The Country School," by Edward L. Henry, Estate of Francis P. Garvan), 143 ("The Old Stile," by John G. Brown, property of John Marshall Phillips)
Lent by Mrs. William E. S. Zuill: page 124 (two upper photographs)

I owe a particular debt of gratitude to Marnie Fahr for her energetic and imaginative assistance in research, to Else Ström for her resourceful help in Washington picture files, and to Deborah Allen for editorial aid; to Cass Canfield who is responsible for the idea of the book; to Russell Lynes, John S. Rudd, Mrs. R. Hawley Truax, William E. Hill, and Mrs. William E. S. Zuill for generous loans of material; to Otis Wiese and Miss Simon of *McCall's*, Miss Grace Mayer of the Museum of the City of New York, Miss Helen Buck of the American Alpine Club, John Springer of RKO, Allen Porter of the Museum of Modern Art, Miss Eileen Thornton of Vassar College, Miss Jean Glasscock of Wellesley College, John H. Detmold of Wells College, and Mrs. Regina Schirmer of *Glamour* for especial helpfulness. I should like to express my appreciation of Arthur W. Rushmore's skill in the production of the book, and to remark that the aid rendered by Frederick Lewis Allen has been beyond calculation.

INDEX

Abbott, Grace, 71
Abolition, 36
Academy Award, 176
Adams, Annette, 113
Adams, Maude, 43
Addams, Jane, 69
Age of Innocence, The, 39
Air raid wardens, 91
Akeley, Carl E., 141
Akeley, Delia, 141
"Alexander's Rag-time Band," 147
"Alice, Where Art Thou Going?" 67
Allen, Frederick Lewis, 151, 153
Allen, Gracie, 174
Allen, Hervey, 170
Altman, B., & Co., 95-97, 99
American Academy of Arts and Sciences, 39
American Airlines, 194
American Committee for Devastated France, 111
American Federation of Labor, 66
American Friends of France, 111
American Mercury, 192
American Red Cross (see Red Cross)
American Women's Association, 111
Amory, Cleveland, 59
Anderson, Jean, 188
Anderson, John Murray, 148, 149
Anderson, Mrs. John Murray, 149
Anderson, Mary, 43
Anna Christie, 175
Annie Get Your Gun, 54
Anthony Adverse, 170
Anthony, Susan B., 36, 62
Anti-suffragists, 64
Appalachian Mountain Club, 135
Archery, 16
Arden, Elizabeth, 198-200
Around the World in Eighty Days, 56
Art, 1, 3, 27, 52, 110, 114, 127, 192, 205, 206
Arthur, Jean, 101
Asch Building, 34
Astor, Carrie, 9
Astor, Mrs. William, 6, 9, 171
Atlantic City Bathing Beauty Contest, 191
Audrey, 39
Authors (see Writers)
Automobiles, 24-26, 58, 72, 74, 90, 119, 142, 151, 213
Aviation, 58, 80, 83, 86-89, 91, 137-140, 194, 215

Baby-sitters, 209
Bacon, Marion, 184
Baedeker guidebooks, 73, 74, 77
Baker, Ray Stannard, 57
Baldwin, Stanley, 171
Baltimore Sun, 40
Bara, Theda, 103
Barnard College, 179
Barretts of Wimpole Street, The, 175
Barrow, Clyde, 164
Barrymore, Ethel, 44
Barrymore family, 44
Barrymore, Lionel, 44, 102
Baseball, 58, 213
Bathing beauties, 103, 191
"Battle Hymn of the Republic, The," 39
Battle With The Slums, The, 32
Baudet, Louise, 45
Baylies, Edmund Lincoln, 8
Beard, Charles A., 71

Beauty, 12, 90, 99, 147, 190-200, 211, 214
Beckwith, Miss, 10
Beer, Thomas, 154
Behees, The Flying, 137
Belasco, David, 44
Bell System, 205
Bellevue Hospital, 41, 42
Belmont, Mrs. August, 5
Belmont, Mrs. O. H. P. (see also Vanderbilt, Mrs. William K.), 7
Bennett, Ann, 118
Bennett, Constance, 77
Bennett, Helen, 197
Benoit, Mrs., 33
Berengaria, 131
Berlin, Irving, 147
Bicycling, 5, 18
Birth control, 57
Bjurstedt, Molla (see also Mallory, Molla), 58, 60
Black Dahlia, The, 163
Blanck, Max, 34, 35
Blanding, Sarah, 112
Blatch, Harriot Stanton, 145
Bly, Nelly, 56
Bobbed-hair Bandit, The, 164
Bobby-soxers, 203
Borden, Lizzie, 160
Boston Cooking-School Cook Book, 39
Boston University, 62
Boucicault, Aubrey, 45
Bow, Clara, 105
Bowling, 204
Boyer, Charles, 177
Bradley, Mary Hastings, 141
Brady, Diamond Jim, 45
Braque, Georges, 183
British Women's Amateur Golf Championship, 173
Brooke, Ellen, 197
Brooklyn Museum, 141
Brown, Mrs. Charles S., 60
Brown, John George, 143
Brown University, 179
Browne, Mary K., 60
Browning, Elizabeth Barrett, 175
Browning, Robert, 175
Bryan, Mildred, 116
Bryan, William Jennings, 66
Bryn Mawr, 179
Buck, Pearl, 108, 170
Buffalo Bill's Wild West Show, 54
Bulkley, Kate, 10
Bundy, May Sutton, 60
Bunny Hug, 147
Burke, Martha Jane (Canary), 55
Burns and Allen, 174
Burlesque (see Showgirls)
Burns, Jackie, 197
Butler, Frank, 54

Café society, 171
Calamity Jane, 55
Camille, 103
Captain January, 39
Captain Jinks of the Horse Marines, 44
Carnegie Tech, 86
Carroll, Earl, 193
Carter, Mrs. Leslie, 44
Castellane, Count de, 29
Castle House, 195
Castle, Irene and Vernon, 195
Cather, Willa, 108
Catt, Carrie Chapman, 36, 62
Cattle Queen of Montana, The, 55
Chagall, Marc, 183
Charleston, 105, 147, 149

Chase, Edna Woolman, 115
Children, 1, 2, 52, 70, 71, 76, 78, 79, 82, 114, 118, 119, 122-129, 166, 176, 203
Children of Divorce, 105
Children's Bureau, 71
Churchill, Lord Randolph, 29
C.I.O., 66
Circus performers, 54, 116, 136, 137, 142
Claire, Ina, 107
Clark, Julia, 140
Cleveland, Anne, 188, 214
Cleveland, Grover, 64, 77
Clewes, Henry, 74
Coaching, 3, 7, 17, 67
Cody, Mabel, 137
Cohn, Fannia M., 68
Colbert, Claudette, 176
College, 16, 21, 37, 62, 69, 112, 121, 127, 135, 178-188, 195, 205, 213
College for Women at Western Reserve, 179
Collett, Glenna, 131
Collier's, 192
Collins, Mrs. Nathaniel, 55
Colorado Mountain Club, 135
Communism, 68
Congress, 62
Cooney, Celia, 164
Cooney, Edward Sebastian, 164
Cooper, Gary, 105
Copland, Aaron, 183
Corbin, Louise, 29
Corio, Ann, 193
Cornell, Katharine, 107, 175
"Country School, The," 37
Crandon, Mrs. L. R. G., 117
Crawford, Joan, 105, 210
Crime, 46, 116, 118, 119, 154-157, 160-164
Croquet, 16, 18
Crothers, Rachel, 111
Curtis, Margaret, 60
Curtis, Miss, 29
Curzon, Lord, 29
Custer, General, 55
Cutler, Roger W., 59

Dague, Walter Glenn, 162
Dancing, 101, 104, 105, 129, 130, 147-150, 152, 153, 171, 183, 195, 200, 207
Dancing Masters of America, 116
Daniels, Bebe, 100
Dark Victory, 177
Darrow, Whitney, Jr., 172, 209
Daudet, Alphonse, 154
Daughter of the Gods, 130
Davis, Bette, 177
Davis, Elmer, 157
Day, Clarence, 170
Day, Robert, 171
DC-4, 194
De Thulstrop, T., 146
Dear Brutus, 107
Delafield, Ann, 200
Deland, Margaret, 39
Depression, 153, 165-169, 171, 205, 209, 214
Didrikson, Babe, 173
Dillinger, John, 164
Divorce, 44, 171
Dohanos, Stevan, 212, 213
"Dollar Princesses," 29
Douglas, Helen Gahagan, 65
Drew, John, 44
Drum-majorettes, 116, 129
Du Barry Success School, 200
Du Bois, Guy Pène, 157

Duchess of Marlborough, 28
Duncan, William, 61
Dunne, Irene, 177
Durbin, Deanna, 211
"Dust Storm, Fifth Avenue," 145
Dwight, James, 20

Eakins, Thomas, 17
Eames, Emma, 47
Earhart, Amelia, 138, 139
Easiest Way, The, 119
East Lynne, 39
Eastman Dry Plate and Film Company, 23
Eastman Kodak Company, 48, 49
Ederle, Gertrude, 131
Edward VIII, King, 171
Elmira College, 179
Elsie Dinsmore, 125
Encyclopedia of Sports, 134
Engelhard, Georgia, 135
Enough Rope, 109
Etiquette, 151
Evans, Dot, 59
Everything Correlates, 188
Explorers, 140, 141

Fair, Miss, 24
"Fairman Rogers Four-in-Hand, The," 17
Farm Security Administration, 128
Farmer, Fannie Merritt, 39
Farrar, Geraldine, 47
Fashion, 3-5, 15, 18-22, 25, 34, 49, 60, 61, 72-74, 92-101, 115, 122, 124, 126, 130, 131, 144, 149, 153, 185, 215
Fay, Larry, 116
Fencing, 58
Ferber, Edna, 109
Fifty Years in Wall Street, 74
Fitch, Clyde, 44, 154
"Fitting Room, The," 202
Fitzgerald, F. Scott, 150
Five Points House of Industry, The, 70
Flappers, 94, 102, 105
Flatiron Building, 145
Flesh and the Devil, The, 104
Floradora, 46
Flying Behees, 137
Folies-Bergère, 45
Fontaine, Joan, 211
Fool There Was, A, 103
Football, 58, 173, 213
Forbes, Mrs. Emery, 120
Fortune-tellers, 117
Four Horsemen of the Apocalypse, The, 103
Fox Films, 130
Fox-trot, 147, 195
Francis, Kay, 101
Frank Leslie's Illustrated Newspaper, 73
Franklin Simon & Co., 144
Frazier, Brenda, 171
Frechette, Evelyn, 164
Frick, Henry Clay, 110
Frohman, Charles, 44

Gable, Clark, 176
"Gang Busters," 164
Gannam, John, 213
Garbo, Greta, 104, 175
Garden, Mary, 47
Gardner, Isabella Stewart, 110
Gardner, Mrs. John L., 110
Gibson, Charles Dana, 12, 22, 64, 65

Gilbert, John, 104
Gilbert, W. S., 118
Gillette, William, 107
Gilman, Charlotte Perkins, 36, 37
Gladwyn, Helen B., 50
Glasgow, Ellen, 108
Glen Ridge primary school, 125
Glyn, Elinor, 40, 105
Goelet, May, 29
Golden Multitudes, 170
Goldman, Emma, 68
Golf, 21, 60, 131, 173
Gone With the Wind, 170
Good Earth, The, 108, 170
Goodman, Benny, 149
Gordon, Louis, 139
Gould, Anna, 29
Gould, Jay, 8
Grace Line, 72
Graham, Florence Nightingale, 198
Graham, Martha, 183
Grapes of Wrath, The, 170, 177
Gray Gables, 77
Gray, Henry Judd, 161
Great American Bandwagon, The,
191
Green, Hetty, 57
Green, William, 66
Griffith, D. W., 102
Grohe, Glenn, 213
G-String Murders, The, 192
Guggenheim Galleries, 192
Guinan, "Texas," 116
Gunther, John, 65

H. Sophie Newcomb College, 179
Hachmeister, Louise, 51
Hall, Rev. Edward Wheeler, 161
Hall, Mrs. Edward Wheeler, 161
Hall-Mills case, 161
Hamilton College, 152
Harkness, Mrs. William, 141
Harper, Ida Husted, 63
Harper's Bazaar, 115, 192
Harper's Weekly, 17, 24, 25, 27, 29-
31, 77, 146, 147, 155
Harriman, Mrs. J. Borden, 66
Harris, Isaac, 34, 35
Harris, Roy, 183
Hart, Irving Harlow, 108
Harvey, Fred, 56
Harvey Girls, 56
"Hatch Family, The," 2
Hawes, Elizabeth, 115
Hayes, Helen, 107, 175
Heart of Maryland, The, 44
Held, John, Jr., 94, 150, 151, 156
Henry, Edward L., 37
Hepburn, Katharine, 177
Herne, Chrystal, 26
Hill, Lucille Eaton, 60
Hillis, Marjorie, 170
Hill's Manual, 152
Hinkley, Albert, 59
History of the Standard Oil Com-
pany, 57
Hitler, 174
Hobby, Oveta Culp, 87
Hockey, 58, 179, 182
Hoffman House, 145
Hollins, Marion, 60
Holm, Eleanor, 131
"Home Life in America," 212, 213
Homer, Winslow, 16
Hoover, Mrs. Herbert, 167
Horton, Mildred McAfee (see also
McAfee, Mildred), 87
Hotchkiss, Hazel V., 58, 60
House of Mirth, The, 39
Housekeeping, 1, 52, 53, 91, 120,
121, 167-169, 208-211
Hovick, Rose Louise, 192
Howe, Julia Ward, 39
Hull House, 69, 71
Huntington, Henry Edwards, 110
Hyde ball, 11
Hyde, James Hazen, 11

Immigration, 30-32, 68, 69
International Ladies Garment
Workers Union, 205

International Suffrage Alliance, 36,
62
Irvin, Rea, 156
Iselin, Mrs. C. Oliver, 5
It Happened One Night, 176
Ives, Charles, 183
I.W.W., 68

Jazz, 147, 149, 150, 183, 207
Jerome, Jennie, 29
Jet Pilot, 198
John Halifax, Gentleman, 39
John Ward, Preacher, 39
Johns Hopkins, 113
Johnson, Eastman, 2
Johnson, Van, 203
Johnston, Mary, 39
Jones, Mother, 68
Judd, Winnie Ruth, 162

Kane, Mrs. DeLancey, 5
Keats, John, 109
Keller, Helen, 38
Kellerman, Annette, 130
Kentucky Derby, 198
Kinsey, Howard, 134
Koch, Carl, 208
Kodak, 23
Kyle, Bee, 136

La Rochefoucauld, Duc de, 29
Labor, 30-32, 34-36, 48, 66, 68, 70,
71, 111, 128, 204, 205
Ladies' Home Journal, 26, 50, 64
Langdon, Marion, 10
Lanvin, 95
Last of Mrs. Cheyney, The, 107
Late George Apley, The, 170
Lathrop, Julia Clifford, 71
Law, Ruth, 83, 140
League of Women Voters, 36
Learning How to Behave, 143
Lee, Gypsy Rose, 192
Leiter, Mary, 29
Lenglen, Suzanne, 134
Lenroot, Katharine F., 71
"Letter from an Unknown
Woman," 167, 168
Liberty, 156
Life, 94, 150, 151
Life at Vassar, 184
Life with Father, 52, 170
Lindbergh, Anne Morrow, 140
Lindbergh, Charles, 140
Listen, the Wind, 140
Little Minister, The, 43
Little Women, 125
Live Alone and Like It, 170
Lonergan, Patricia Burton, 161
Lonergan, Wayne, 161
Longworth, Alice Roosevelt, 67
Longworth, Nicholas, 67
Loos, Anita, 102
Lord & Taylor, 94
Lost Lady, A, 108
Louise, 47
Love, 104
Love Affair, 177
Love, Bessie, 100
Love, Harry, 163
Love, Helen Wills, 163
Lowell, Amy, 109
Loy, Myrna, 176
Luce, Clare Boothe, 65
Lucky Strike cigarettes, 154
Lynd, Robert S. and Helen Merrell,
119, 177, 201

Mack Sennett Bathing Beauties, 103
Male and Female, 103
Mallory, Molla (see also Bjurstedt,
Molla), 58, 134
Margery, 117
Marinettes, 84
Marlborough, Duchess of, 28
Marlowe, Julia, 43
Marmon car, 25
Marquand, John P., 170
Marquand Pavillion, 41

Marriage, 1, 2, 12, 13, 29, 36, 37,
52, 56, 82, 153, 171, 176, 191, 194,
205, 209, 213, 215
Marshall, James, 56
Martha Washington Hotel, 145
Maxixe, 149
Maxwell, Elsa, 65
Mazamas, 135
McAfee, Mildred (see also Horton,
Mildred McAfee), 85
McBride, Mary Margaret, 172
McCall patterns, 4, 5, 95, 96, 98
McCall's (see also *Queen of Fash-*
ion, The), 4, 29, 52, 81, 96, 98,
167, 168
McClure, S. S., 57
McClure's, 57
McCormick, Anne O'Hare, 111
McKee, Joseph, 139
McKinley, William, 154
Meadows, Alberta, 162
Mellon, Andrew W., 110
Merman, Ethel, 54
Merry Widow, The, 104
Merz, Charles, 191
Metropolitan Opera, 11
Michaux Club, 18
Middletown, 119
Middletown in Transition, 177, 201
Milholland, Inez, 62
Millay, Edna St. Vincent, 109
Miller, Kenneth Hayes, 202
Miller Sisters, 46
Millman, Bird, 137
Mills, Mrs. James, 161
Milwaukee *Journal,* 154
Minnesota *Daily,* 182
Miss America, 191
Mitchell, Margaret, 170
Mitchell, Maria, 37
Mitchell, Mattie, 29
Mlle Fifi, 45
Models, 160, 191, 196, 197, 213
Modjeska, 43
Moisant, Mathilda, 140
Montgomery, Robert, 105
Moody's Investor's Survey, 154
Moore, Alexander P., 45
Morgan, Anne, 111
Morgan, J. P. & Co., 140
Morgan, J. Pierpont, 110, 111
Morganstern, C. William, 116
Morning Glory, 177
Morrow, Anne, 140
Morrow, Dwight, 140
Mother's Day, 204
Mott, Frank Luther, 170
Mott, Lucretia, 36
Mount Holyoke, 179
Mountain-climbing, 135
Mountaineers, The, 135
Mourning, 144
Movies, 65, 77, 81, 83, 100-106, 116,
130, 148, 151, 171, 175-177, 209-211
Mozee, Phoebe Annie Oakley, 54
Mrs. Astor's Horse, 131
Muhlenberg Branch of the New
York Public Library, 114
Mulrooney, Edward P., 118
Murray, Arthur, 195
Murray, Mae, 104
Murray, Philip, 66
My Antonia, 108

Nation, Carry, 155
National Academy of Sciences, 113
National Woman Suffrage Associa-
tion, 36, 62, 63
National Women's Track and Field
Championship, 173
Nazimova, 103
Nazis, 174
Neptune's Daughter, 130
Nesbit, Evelyn, 160
Nestor, Agnes, 68
Nethersole, Olga, 154
New Directions Press, 183
New Haven Normal School of
Gymnastics, 112
New Jersey Senate Chamber, 166
New York City Hall, 165
New York Coaching Club, 17
New York Hat, The, 102

New York Herald, 5, 18
New York Public Library, 114
New York Skating Club, 19
New York Telephone Company, 51
New York Times, 9, 10, 111
New York World, 56
New York World's Fair, 131, 192
New Yorker, The, 129, 156, 158, 170-
172, 192, 209
Newman, Pauline M., 70
Nichols, L. V. B., 208
Nieman-Marcus, 202
Night clubs, 116, 171
Nineteenth Amendment, 62, 151
Nixon, Marian, 101
North to the Orient, 140
Now I'll Tell, 176
Nudism, 170
Nursing, 41, 42, 48, 82, 83, 85, 91,
142, 194

O Pioneers, 108
Oakley, Annie, 54
O'Connor, Peggy, 197
Of Human Bondage, 177
"Old Stile, The," 143
Olympic Games, 173
One of Ours, 108
O'Neill, Eugene, 107
Only Yesterday, 151
Opera, 45, 47
Orford, Earl of, 29
Osborn, Robert, 206, 207, 215
Oscars, 177
Our Dancing Daughters, 105
Outerbridge, Miss, 20
Outlook, The, 60
Owen, Ruth Bryan, 66

Packard Motor Car Company, 48
Padlocks of 1927, The, 116
Palmer, Alice Freeman, 37
Paramount Theatre, 149, 203
Parent Teachers Association, 103
Parker, Bonnie, 164
Parker, Dorothy, 109
Partisan Review, The, 183
Patou, 94
Patterson, Nan, 46
Paxton, William M., 13
Peck, Annie Smith, 135
Perils of Pauline, The, 104
Perkins, Frances, 66
Perkins Institute for the Blind, 38
Pershing, General, 83
Philadelphia Skating and Humane
Society, 19
Philadelphia Story, The, 177
Phillips, Clara, 162
Photography, 23, 86
Pickford, Mary, 83, 102, 103
Pinafore, 45
Pioneers, 54, 56, 143
Plunder, 104
Poems of Passion, 40
Policewomen, 118
Politics, 1, 7, 36, 62-68, 71, 88, 113,
121, 155, 159
Pollyanna, 102
Polo, 58
Pope, Frances Eaton, 42
Possessed, 105
Post, Emily, 151
Powell, William, 176
Powers, John Robert, 196, 197
Printers' Ink, 154
Progressive National Convention,
62
Prohibition, 116, 151, 155-159, 171
Proper Bostonians, The, 59
Prostitution, 119, 154
Psychoanalysis, 172
Pulitzer Prize, 108
Purtle, Ethel, 142
Putnam, Mrs. George Palmer (see
also Earhart, Amelia), 139

Quaker Girl, The, 107
Queen Christina, 104
Queen of Fashion, The (see also
McCall's), 4-6, 18, 21, 53, 123

Queen of the Night Club, 116
Quimby, Harriet, 140

Radcliffe College, 38, 179
Radio, 106, 118, 140, 174, 206, 213
"Railroads on Trial," 57
Red Cross, 66, 83, 88, 90, 91
Red Fairy Book, The, 125
Red Lamp, 108
Reich, Susan Flora, 163
Reinhart, C. S., 27
Réjane, Mme, 11
Religion, 62, 151, 155, 161, 201
Remington Rand, 49
Renée fashions, 97
Repeal, 159
Reporters, 56, 63, 111, 174, 180, 182
Resor, Mrs. Stanley, 115
Richards, Laura E., 39
Riis, Jacob, 32, 33, 70
Rinehart, Mary Roberts, 108
Rita, 29
Roche, Josephine, 113
Rockefeller Institute for Medical
  Research, 113
Rogers, Edith Nourse, 65
Rogers, Fairman, 17
Roller skating, 19
Romantic Comedians, The, 108
Roosevelt, Eleanor, 67, 167, 171
Roosevelt, Franklin Delano, 67
Roosevelt, Theodore, 57
Rose, Billy, 131
Rose, Carl, 129
Rouault, Georges, 183
Roxburghe, Duchess of, 29
Royal Geographical Society, 141
Rubinstein, Helena, 199
"Rumors of War," 82
Russell, Lillian, 45
Russell Sage Foundation, 69

Sabin, Mrs. Charles, 159
Sabin, Florence, 113
Sage, Anna, 164
Sage, Mrs. Russell, 69
St. Paul Pioneer Press, 46
Sands, Anna, 20
Sanger, Margaret, 57
Santa Fe Railroad, 56
Santa Rosa, 72
Sapho, 154
Sargent, John Singer, 13, 14
Satterlee, Herbert L., 67
Satterlee, Mrs. Herbert L., 67
Saturday Evening Post, 209
Schaeffer, Mead, 212, 213
Schlesinger, Arthur M., 143, 151
Schmitt, Katherine M., 51
Schneiderman, Rose, 68
Schroeder, Irene, 162
Schwab, Charles M., 50
Scientists, 86, 113, 141
Scott, Blanche, 140
Scott, Orlando, 163
Sears, Eleanora, 58-60
Secretaries, 49, 50, 213
Sennett, Mack, 103
Servants, 31, 32, 53, 208
Sewing, 52, 95, 98, 121, 209
Shahn, Ben, 183
Shame of the Cities, The, 57
Shaver, Dorothy, 94, 115
Shaw, Anna Howard, 62
Shepard, Mrs. Finley, 69
Sheridan, Ann, 210
Sherry's, 11

Sholes, Christopher, 49
Short, Elizabeth, 163
Sierra Club, 135
Simpson, Wallis Warfield, 171
Sinatra, Frank, 203
Since Yesterday, 153
Sing Sing, 161
Singers, 45, 47, 48, 129, 130, 177
Sitting Pretty, 209
Skating, 19, 80
Sketch Book, The, 193
Skiing, 80, 173
Sloan, John, 145
Sloane, The Misses, 5
Smedley, W. T., 3, 18, 82
Smith College, 135, 179
Smoking, 154
Snow, Carmel, 115
Snyder, Albert, 161
Snyder, Ruth, 161
So Big, 109
Social Ladder, The, 12
Social Work, 57, 69-71, 111, 128, 186,
  214
"Soria Moria Castle," 125
Spanish American War, 82
SPARS, 87
Speakeasies, 156, 157
Spiritualism, 117
Sports, 5, 16, 18-22, 24-26, 48, 54,
  58-61, 74, 77, 79, 80, 100, 112, 130-
  135, 173, 179-182, 198, 204, 207,
  213
Squash, 58, 59
Stammers, Kay, 132
Standard Oil Company, 57
Stanton, Elizabeth Cady, 36
Stark, Mabel, 142
Starr, Frances, 119
Steffens, Lincoln, 57
Steinbeck, John, 170, 177
Sterling, Alexa, 60
Stewart, James, 177
Stickney, Dorothy, 52
Stimson, Julia C., 83
Stinson, Katherine, 140
Stinson, Marjorie, 140
Stockdale, Mrs. Artie, 118
Stokes, Mr. and Mrs. I. N. Phelps,
  13, 14
Stork Club, 171
Stratton, Dorothy C., 87
Streeter, Ruth Cheney, 87
Streets of Paris, 192
Strip-teasers, 192, 193
Strong, Kate, 10
Stryker, Lloyd P., 152
Stutz Bearcat, 26
Stutz, Wilmer, 139
Suffrage (see Women's rights)
Suffrage parade of 1915, 62
Sullivan, Anne Mansfield, 38
Sullivan, Mary, 118
Sun bathing, 185
Sutton, May G., 60
Swanson, Gloria, 103
Sweatshops, 31, 34, 35, 70, 71
Swimming, 5, 22, 75, 77, 80, 130,
  131, 207

Tale of Two Cities, A, 39
Talleyrand-Perigord, Marquis de, 29
Tango, 149
Tarbell, Ida M., 57
Taylor, Annie Edson, 136
Taylor, Ruth, 101
"Tea Leaves," 13

Teaching, 3, 37, 38, 48, 51, 69-71,
  110, 112-114, 121, 135, 151, 195,
  201
Telephones, 51
Television, 106, 213
Tellegen, Lou, 47
Temperance, 36, 155, 156, 159
Temple, Shirley, 176
Tennis, 20, 21, 58, 60, 61, 100, 132-
  134, 180
Thaw, Harry Kendall, 160
Theatre, 26, 43-46, 48, 61, 65, 102,
  107, 111, 116, 119, 148, 171, 175,
  191
Theatre Guild, 107
Thin Man, The, 176
Thompson, Dorothy, 174
Thompson, J. Walter, 115
Thompson, Lydia, 190
Three Weeks, 40, 47
Thropp, Frances, 190
Thurber, James, 170
Tittle, Walter, 147
To Have and To Hold, 39
Todd, John, 178
Tracy, Spencer, 176
Travers, William R., 74
Triangle Fire, 34, 35
Triangle Waist Company, 34, 35, 70
Troy Female Seminary, 37
Tulane University, 179
Turkey Trot, 147
Turnure, Miss, 10
Tuxedo Horse Show, 22
Twiddle Twaddle, 46
Two-step, 152
Typewriter, 49

Uncle Tom's Cabin, 39, 170
United Airlines, 194
United States (Baedeker), 77
U.S. Army Nurse Corps, 83, 85
U.S. Brewers Foundation, 212
U.S. Naval Air Station, 85
U.S. Navy Nurse Corps, 85
University of Kentucky, 112
University of Minnesota, 179, 182
University of Pennsylvania, 59
Untamed, 105

Valentino, Rudolph, 103
Vanderbilt ball, 9, 10
Vanderbilt, Consuelo, 28
Vanderbilt, Cornelius, 3, 9
Vanderbilt, William K., 9, 10, 24, 28
Vanderbilt, Mrs. William K., 9, 24,
  28
Varesi, Mlle, 11
Variety, 192
Vassar, A Second Glance, 188
Vassar Banjo Club, 180
Vassar College, 37, 109, 112, 127,
  153, 178-180, 182-184, 186-188
Vassar, Matthew, 178, 180
Vassar Summer Institute for Family
  and Community Living, 187
Verne, Jules, 56
Versailles, 11
Victoria Regina, 175
Vogue, 94, 95, 97, 98, 115, 147
Voice, The, 203
Voice of the People, The, 108
Von Stroheim, Eric, 104

WAAC, 85-87
Walden, 39

Waldo, Ruth, 115
Walker, Jimmy, 131
Walker, Stanley, 131
Wallach, Mrs. Barger, 20
Walter, 117
Walter, Eugene, 119
Wanamaker, 98
War, 66, 82-91, 94, 118, 151, 154,
  161, 186, 187, 192, 209
War Production Board, 88
Warner Brothers, 116
Washington, George, 131
Washington Square Players, 107
WAVES, 85, 87
W.C.T.U., 155
Webb, Clifton, 209
Webb, Madeline, 163
Wellesley College, 21, 37, 179-181
Wellesley Prelude, 180
Wells College, 16, 185
Wenzell, A. B., 19, 72
Western Reserve, 179
Wethered, Joyce, 131
Wharton, Edith, 39
White, Mrs. Frank, 10
White House, 51
White, Newton, 85
White, Pearl, 104
White, Stanford, 160
White Steamer, 25
Whitney, Gertrude Vanderbilt, 110
Whitney Museum, 110
Whitney Studio Club, 110
Whitney Studio Gallery, 110
Wightman, Mrs. George W., 58, 60
Wilcox, Ella Wheeler, 40
Willard, Emma, 37
Willard, Frances, 155
Willebrandt, Mabel Walker, 159
Wills, Helen, 132-134
Wilson, Woodrow, 71
Windsor, Duke and Duchess of, 171
Winter, William, 44
Winton, Alexander, 25
Woman and Economics, 36
Woman in Red, 164
Woman of Affairs, A, 104
Woman Rebel, The, 57
Woman's Crusade, 155
Women's Christian Temperance
  Union, 155
Women's clubs, 151, 202
Women's College at Brown Uni-
  versity, 179
Women's Organization for Prohi-
  bition Reform, 159
Women's rights, 7, 36, 37, 54, 62-66,
  68, 94, 145, 151, 186, 205
Women's Trade Union League, 68,
  70, 111
Woollcott, Alexander, 147, 152
Worth, Barbara, 100
Writers, 36, 39, 40, 48, 56, 57, 63,
  65, 102, 108, 109, 111, 140, 148,
  150, 170, 174, 192
Wynekoop, Alice Lindsay, 163

Yeoman (F), 83, 84
Young, Frank Thomas, 46
Young, Loretta, 100
Ypsilanti Normal School, 152

Zaharias, Mrs. George, 173
Zaza, 44
Ziegfeld Follies, 107
Zworykin, Vladimir, 106